25 Ways To Keep Your Child Safe, Healthy and Successful:

Lessons from a School Counselor

Michelle Farias

TRAFFORD
PUBLISHING

Note for Librarians: A cataloguing record for this book is available from
Library and Archives Canada at
www.collectionscanada.ca/amicus/index-e.html
ISBN 1-4120-6097-4

Printed on paper with minimum 30%
recycled fibre.
Trafford's print shop runs on "green energy" from solar, wind and other
environmentally-friendly power sources.

Offices in Canada, USA, Ireland and UK
This book was published on-demand in cooperation with Trafford
Publishing. On-demand publishing is a unique process and service of
making a book available for retail sale to the public taking advantage
of on-demand manufacturing and Internet marketing. On-demand
publishing includes promotions, retail sales, manufacturing, order
fulfilment, accounting and collecting royalties on behalf of the author.

Book sales for North America and international:
Trafford Publishing, 6E–2333 Government St.,
Victoria, BC v8t 4p4 CANADA
phone 250 383 6864 (toll-free 1 888 232 4444)
fax 250 383 6804; email to orders@trafford.com
Book sales in Europe:
Trafford Publishing (uk) Ltd., Enterprise House, Wistaston Road
Business Centre,
Wistaston Road, Crewe, Cheshire cw2 7rp United Kingdom
phone 01270 251 396 (local rate 0845 230 9601)
facsimile 01270 254 983; orders.uk@trafford.com
Order online at:
trafford.com/05-0998

More in depth information about the topics discussed in this book may be found in the following booklets.

Booklets and CDs

Children and Stress
Children and Substance Abuse
Children and Academic Success
The Parent/Child Relationship
Children and Personal Safety
Children and Eating Disorders
Children and the Internet
Children and Emotional Health
Teaching Children about Sexuality
Adults and Stress

Log on to
www.borderlandsbooks.com
(keyword: Michelle Farias)
for ordering information.

Disclaimer

The information shared by Michelle Farias is for educational purposes, and it is not a substitute for professional counseling or medical advice. This publication is sold with the understanding that the author is not engaged in rendering medical, health or any other type of professional services in the book. The reader of this publication should consult with a mental health or medical professional for concerns related to his or her (or his or her child's) specific situation or condition. The author specifically disclaims all responsibility for any liability, loss, or risk, personal or otherwise, which is incurred as a consequence, directly or indirectly, from the use and application of any contents of this book.

TABLE OF CONTENTS

INTRODUCTION

"I don't know what to do with my son anymore," said an anguished voice on the other end of the phone. "He is in alternative school for using drugs on campus. We went to court, and the judge ordered him to do community service; my son did not care. I take him to counseling, but he will get out of the car on the way to the appointments. I take him to drug awareness classes, and he does not participate. I have taken everything out of his room, and he is not allowed to leave the house, but he still sneaks out at night. What else am I suppose to do? Tell me what to do now?" How many times have you reached the point as a parent where you wonder, "What am I suppose to do now?" As a school counselor, I often get calls similar to this from frustrated parents. Parents reach the point with their children where they do not know what to do anymore. They have tried everything they know to get their children to make the best choices, and nothing is working. Parenting children today is more challenging than ever because so many outside forces influence the healthy development of children. Additionally, parents are spending less time each day with their children as they work to meet the demands of societal expectations and a changing economy. Parenting healthy children today, without the help of outside resources, is increasingly difficult. Consequently, parents are seeking a partnership with their children's schools to help ensure that their children will have the best chance for a healthy and successful childhood. The demands of today's society require that parents and schools develop a strong partnership to help children maneuver the challenges of today's world for their own suc-

7

cess and well being.

The issues facing children today require that parents and schools work together to help children achieve success. Advances in technology and the increasingly fast-paced demands of society have accelerated the problems that children encounter. Thanks to the media, music and the Internet children of all ages are being exposed more intensely to violence, sex, drugs and new attitudes. Many children are influenced by these mediums to make unhealthy choices for coping with their problems. Children are encouraged to escape from their problems by using drugs or confiding in strangers on the Internet. Children are being encouraged to not trust parents and rebel against adults. These influences are interfering with children's abilities to make healthy choices, achieve success and live happy lives.

The statistics for today's children are startling. According to the 2003 Youth Risk Behavior Surveillance report from the Department of Health and Human Services, 74.9% of high school students have tried alcohol; 40.2% of students have tried marijuana; 46.7% of students have had sexual intercourse; and 16.9% of students have considered suicide. These statistics are alarming, and they show that millions of today's children are in crisis and need help. Children usually do not suddenly develop problems in school or at home. Problems often grow and develop over time. The signs of distress can be so minor that they go unnoticed. These minor incidents can occur in early childhood and continue to build over time. Eventually, the minor incidences culminate into a major problem—usually in adolescence—that catches parents by surprise. The major problems can include drug use, pregnancy, school failure, runaway, depression, suicide, or a host of other life-changing issues. These problems usually occur in high school, but they are being seen more and more in middle and elementary school. These are the problems that are endangering the health and safety of children and creating barriers to their success. These problems, though, can be prevented when parents and schools work together to guide and prepare children to be successful adults in society.

The choice to be a parent is one of the most powerful decisions one person can make for another because a parent has a profound impact on a child's life. The choice to be a parent is a commitment to guide a child towards success as an adult. This is not a choice to be taken lightly. A parent is the filter through which the child learns about the world—learns about trust and mistrust, right and wrong, and acceptance and rejection. When a parent gives a child the experience of a loving, nurturing, safe and involved childhood, the child is given the opportunity to succeed. When these conditions are not present in childhood, the child struggles to survive. Parents often forget the power they have over their child's experience of the world. Parents are the primary guardians in keeping their children safe and healthy. Parents are the gatekeepers on their child's road to success or failure.

Schools are the primary place where children experience success or failure. Children's feelings toward school range from love to indifference to hate. These attitudes are a reflection of the amount of success a child finds in school. It is not a gamble for which experience a child will have. A child's experience in school is a direct result of the quality of partnership that exists between the parent and the school. Success in school is no longer solely a result of how well a student learns and how hard a student studies. A student's success in school is now influenced by how well he or she copes with problems and resists peer pressures combined with having good study habits. Parents provide the primary guidance in teaching their children the tools needed to make healthy choices and achieve success. Schools enhance the parents' teachings. All children should have the opportunity to work for success while living safe and healthy lives. Parents and schools must work as partners to create this opportunity for each child.

There are simple things parents can do to keep their children safe, healthy and successful. This book is a series of lessons to help parents successfully guide their children through childhood. These lessons have been derived from my many years of experience working as an educator and seeing what is missing for children who struggle. All children can find success with the right preparation and intervention from both parents and the schools. Some of the lessons are common sense, and some are information of which parents may not be aware. They all, though, impact a child's ability to succeed. Only one or two issues presented in this book might affect some children and others might be struggling with many issues. You might read a lesson that is not relevant for you now, but it might become meaningful in a few years. Use this book as a resource for gaining insight into the struggles that children face today. If a lesson grabs your attention and you wonder if it relates to your child, pursue the issue further by consulting with your school counselor or another resource. As a parent, you have the power to guide your child through a safe, healthy and successful adolescence. Learning how to handle the issues that might affect your child today or in the future will give you the tools you need to help your child achieve success and live a happy and fulfilled life.

Note: The term "parent" is used throughout this book, and it encompasses any adult who has accepted the responsibility of raising and nurturing a child towards adulthood.

1

Maintain a Healthy Relationship with Your Child

"My mother doesn't even care about me. All she cares about is her boyfriends. She doesn't pay any attention to me. I don't care if I pass or not."

A thirteen-year old girl who was struggling in school expressed this pain to me. Her focus was not on being successful in school; her time and energy were focused on her unhealthy relationship with her mother. She did not feel her mother cared about her, so she did not care about herself either. This child is facing a lifetime of struggles. Your relationship with your child is the foundation for all of his or her other relationships, choices, and behaviors. Your actions and words affect your child from the day he or she is born if not before. Your beliefs and character are the primary models for your child. You have the power to guide your child towards success or set him or her up for failure. You are the most powerful influence in your child's life, and this power cannot be taken for granted. You are the force in your child's life that has the most impact on whether or not he or she will be successful.

Your relationship with your child requires much energy. It is not something that can be maintained without effort. The time you spend with your child is gold. Your child learns about the world through you. Your child's perception of the world is shaped based on his or her relationship with you. If your child learns that you are reliable, trustworthy and safe, then your child will have faith that the world is a reliable, trustworthy and safe place. This is important when a child begins building relationships with others. Children who trust their parents are more easily able to trust their teachers and excel in school.

You establish trust with your child by being consistent with your behavior. Extreme changes in moods or actions can be very frightening and confusing for a child. This is one reason why children of alcoholics have such a hard time developing healthy relationships. They learned from their alcoholic parents to never let their guard down and feel safe. They never know what to expect from their alcoholic parents. If you struggle with addictions or mood swings, seek professional help for the sake of your child as well as your own well-being.

You establish trust with your child by being present. Your physical and emotional presence creates a safety net for your child. He or she knows that if there is a problem, there is someone available for comfort and safety. When your child trusts that you will be there for him or her, then your child can learn to trust that others can be depended on for help as well. If your child does not develop that trust, then he or she will not allow others, like teachers, to help him or her. Your physical presence requires that you spend time with your child. It is hard to build a relationship with your child if you are a workaholic or you are busy with other activities. Your physical presence with your child is essential to building a healthy relationship.

Andres, a likable fourth grader, does well in his schoolwork, yet his behavior is a problem. The teacher and the counselor met with his mom to discuss what strategies could be used to help Andres be more successful. Several interventions were tried, but he continued to get into trouble. Finally, Andres confided in the counselor that he misses his father. Even though his father lives at home, Andres never sees him. Andres further explained that his father is a lawyer and he is always at work. Andres has the newest toys and the latest computer games, but his dad is never around to play with him. Andres finally admitted, "I would rather have no toys than no dad." Andres had been trying to get his dad's attention through his misbehavior, and, unfortunately, the dad still did not get the message.

Children thrive on the attention they receive from their parents. When the attention is lacking, a void is created within children that they desperately try to fill—often in unhealthy ways. A healthy relationship with your child requires your physical presence as well as your emotional presence. Your emotional presence requires that you are able to really listen to your child when you spend time together, and you are not distracted by other activities. Listening to your child does not involve lecturing. It means putting aside your need to express opinions or give advice and just listen. Empty your mind of the words you want to say, and stay present. Hear what your child is sharing. Try to understand what your child is feeling and expressing. When children believe they are being heard, they are more willing to talk and share thoughts, fears and experiences which strengthen the parent/child relationship. Children need to know that if they have a problem you are the one person to whom they can turn for empathy and support. A child's home must be the safe place to be when life has become difficult, and you must be the safe person to be with him or her.

You establish trust with your child by giving him or her positive comments and feedback. Parents who try to motivate or discipline their children through hurtful comments are only chipping away at a fragile ego. Children learn how they fit into the world by how their parents perceive them.

Kendra was told daily by her father that she was stupid. She struggled to graduate from high school, and she did not even attempt to go to college until she was in her late 20's. She now has a masters degree, but she still struggles with the belief that she is stupid.

The words of parents are powerful shapers in a child's life. Comments such as, "I love you, but I don't like you… You are just like your father …I wish you were never born…Why can't you be more like your sister?…You aren't smart enough to go to college," will ring in a child's head for years. Even if comments are said in a joking manner, children can take them seriously. These comments cause a child to struggle with feeling good about him or herself, and they make being successful in school more difficult. I have had parents tell me in front of their children that the children will never amount to anything, and meeting with school officials is a waste of the parents' time. Children internalize their parents' beliefs, and they accept the beliefs as truth, which affects self-esteem and healthy development. On the contrary, comments such as, "You are so smart. . . I am so proud of you. . . You can achieve whatever you want to achieve," are much more life-affirming and strengthening. Children who grow up with these comments have a better chance of being successful in school.

Parents will often compare their child with the accomplishments of another sibling or peer in an effort to make him or her try harder.

> *Lee was excited because his dad was taking him to his play class. He usually went with his mom, but his dad took the morning off to be with him. During the class, Lee's father was constantly comparing him to the other children. "Look at that kid. He climbs so much better than you. That kid can run faster than you. You need to learn to keep up with them." Lee is five years old.*

This strategy of comparing your child to another child will backfire. When children are compared negatively with others, their self-esteem is diminished because they are being told that they are not as good as someone else. They are left feeling worthless. Look for positive ways to motivate your child. Praise what your child does well, and work with him or her to improve in weak areas. Children know if they are not as good as someone else, and they do not need a parent to reinforce this belief. Yet, you can be supportive in your child's efforts to improve in weak areas. All children have areas in which they can excel. Discover what these are, and encourage your child to explore his or her potential. Your child will struggle with some tasks or activities, but when he or she learns in what areas he or she can excel, your child's self-esteem will grow. This will benefit your child in the school setting where students often compete with each other. Your child will be proud of what he or she can do well and will be positive about working to improve in weaker areas.

Maintaining a healthy relationship with children involves setting boundaries. Children are children and parents are parents. A parent's role is not to be a friend. Many parent/child relationships become unhealthy because parents try to be their child's friend. This can include allowing children to participate in activities that are not appropriate such as drinking. When parents relinquish their role as a parent in favor of being their children's friend, children are left confused and lost.

> *Alyssa has the coolest parents. They let her and her friends drink at the house every weekend. Alyssa's mom told her, "I know you are going to drink, so I would rather you drink at home." Her friends' parents have strict rules against drinking, and her friends are amazed that Alyssa's parents allow drinking. The kids have learned that drinking can be dangerous—especially to growing teenage bodies—but if Alyssa's parents think it is okay, then it must be okay.*

Children need their parents to be parents. They need to have the structure and rules that parents provide. All children say they want parents who let them do whatever they want, but the truth is children depend on parents to keep them safe as they make their way through childhood. Parents who do not accept the responsibility of guiding their children and setting limits are endangering their children physically and emotionally. Do not be hesitant about setting limits and enforcing them. Children crave the safety this structure provides.

Many parent/child relationships become unhealthy because the parents' personal problems become the children's problems. Children do not need to know details about their parents' finances or marital problems.

> *Maria cannot concentrate in school. Her mom told her last week that her dad had had an affair. The affair is over, but her mom is having trouble trusting him. Maria's mom told her she was thinking of getting a divorce. Maria is angry with her dad, and she is worried about her mom. School seems so unimportant when your family is falling apart.*

Parents are the adults; children are the children. Children do not have the emotional maturity or experience to listen to their parents' adult problems. Parents need to have an adult friend or a mental health professional in whom to confide, because children should not be put in the position of being the confidant. They do not have the resources to cope with adult problems as well as their own.

Yet, even if parents try to shield their children from problems, children can still be affected by the problems of their parents. If a child's parent or family member is divorced, incarcerated, ill, stressed, experiencing emotional difficulties, or having other problems, the child will be affected. This makes it difficult for the child to concentrate in school and do well, and it causes emotional stress for the child. If your family is going through a challenging time, you might want to consider giving your child the opportunity to talk to a counselor. Children are influenced by the problems of their parents, and a mental health professional can teach children the skills needed to cope with stress and difficult family situations.

The first step in your child achieving success in school is in the quality of his or her relationship with you. Your child's understanding of healthy relationships will stem from having positive experiences with you. This will benefit your child in the school setting as he or she develops strong relationships with adults and peers with whom he or she interacts. Your relationship with your child is the foundation on which your child develops a healthy sense of self and a positive belief about his or her potential. You can give your child the tools necessary to be successful by developing a strong and healthy relationship with him or her that will prepare your child for success.

2

Value Education

Jason is frustrated. He is failing math, and if he does not improve in his grades, he might have to go to summer school. "Why do I have to know this stuff?" he asked. "What good is it going to do for me to learn all of this? I don't need to graduate. I can get a good job with my friend's dad."

Students make these comments to me every year. They usually emerge when a student is struggling to learn a difficult concept or when a student is failing. Learning is hard. A few students can sail through school without much effort, but most students struggle with at least one subject if not more. It is in these times of struggle that students begin to wonder if the hard work is worth it. Is it worth the pain, effort and frustration to learn? What is the point of sitting in classes all day and doing more homework at night? "Surely," students wonder, "there is more to life than this."

There is more to life than school. Yet, school is the vehicle needed to get to the "more." Education will open unlimited doors for students, and the possibilities are endless. There was a time when a person could make an adequate living without a high school diploma. Eventually, a high school diploma was needed to get a job with a good future. Now, some kind of college or training is essential for success. The U.S. Department of Education (www.ed.gov) publishes statistics each year showing that people with a college education earn significantly more than people with only a high school education. Many students do not understand the reality of needing an education to achieve success while they are plowing their way through school. Students often go to school each day because it is expected of them. They do not see the bigger picture of the importance of their education. They will not truly understand the value of their education unless parents teach it to them through words and actions.

You can teach your child that school is important. Your child is more likely to remain in school and be successful if you teach him or her the value of education. If you do not have a diploma, you can still instill in your child the importance of graduating from high school and continuing on to college or a training program to develop a career. You must frequently share with your child that an education is the ticket to success. Your child may choose a career where a college degree or training program is not necessary, but he or she still needs to be encouraged to earn a degree or certification beyond high school for support and to create more options.

Julie: I don't want to go to college. I want to cut hair. I don't need an education to cut hair.

Dad: I didn't want to go to college either. When I was in high school, all I wanted to do was work on cars. I am working on cars now, but my boss is on my back all day long to work harder. I wish I had gone to college so that I could do something else. At least I could have learned about starting my own business. Then, I would be my own boss. But, I am stuck now, working for this guy. Go to college. You can always cut hair after you graduate. But, at least you will have other choices if you change your mind.

People are more successful when they have a variety of options open to them for their careers. Education creates these options. Set high expectations for your child when he or she is young. Tell your child that you expect for him or her to graduate from high school and continue with education to earn a degree or certification. Let your child know that dropping out of school is not an option. If you set your standards high, your child will rise to the expectation.

You teach your child the value of education by showing respect for the educators. If you convey to your child the message that "Teachers don't know what they are doing," you are setting your child up for problems relating to his or her teachers. Teachers generally choose to teach because they value learning, and they enjoy children. Teachers want your child to be successful, and they work hard to learn the knowledge and skills needed to guide children towards success. Teachers have to graduate from college, and in many states pass state exams, before they can be called a teacher. Even after teachers have graduated from college and started their careers, many teachers continue on with school to earn more degrees and/or receive more training.

Richard: My teacher is so dumb. She is boring and she doesn't even know what she is talking about. I know more than she does.

Mom: Richard, your teacher went to college to earn a degree so that she could be your teacher. If you are bored in her class, talk to her about what you are feeling, or I can talk to her. But, you must treat her with respect because she has earned it.

When you respect the efforts that educators have made in order to be your child's teacher, your child will learn to respect them as well. A child is more likely to be successful in school if he or she respects the teachers who are there everyday to help him or her learn.

You teach your child that you value education by supporting good attendance. Good attendance in school is essential for your child to be successful. Students who are absent miss out on direct teaching and guidance from the teachers. Students who are absent have to catch up with the work they missed in addition to completing the work currently being taught. Students will get sick or have emergencies, and these absences are understandable. Students, though, who are frequently absent because they do not feel like going to school or because their families need them at home to baby-sit or work are at-risk for failing in school. Teach your child the value of education by having high expectations for good attendance.

You teach your child the value of education by getting involved in his or her school. Get to know your child's teachers at the beginning of the school year. Do not wait until there is a problem before you meet the teachers. Attend school functions including Open House. Introduce yourself to the teachers, the counselors and the administrators. Let the school officials know that you care about your child's education, and you want to be involved. If you do not speak English or you have a disability that makes participating in school functions difficult, ask the school for assistance. Schools have the resources needed to assist with these challenges. Join the parent/teacher organization, and volunteer for school functions or activities if you have the time. When you volunteer or join school organizations, you will meet parents who have children the same age as yours. These parents can be a good support system for you and a good resource, as they understand the experience of raising a child the same age as your child. It is easier to be involved with your child's school if you know the other parents. Parents who are actively involved in their children's school send a message to their children that education is important. More specifically, their children's education is important. Parental involvement in schools improves student achievement. When parents are involved in their children's school, their children are more likely to feel connected to the school and be successful.

Parents need to be partners in their children's education. Show your child that you value education. Teach your child why learning is important, show respect for educators, and take time to become involved in your child's school. You are a partner in your child's education, and your involvement will have an impact on his or her success. Set high educational standards for your child, and give him or her the support needed to reach those standards.

3

Create a Positive Attitude Towards School

Min: I don't want to go back to school. School is so boring. I want to stay home and have fun.

Mom: I know the start of school can be a struggle, but remember how much fun you have in school. You get to see your friends everyday and eat lunch with them. And, you get to go on field trips and join the reader's club.

Min: That's true. I guess school is okay. I just don't want to get up early!

Back to School sales begin emerging in mid-summer. The bold, bright signs hanging throughout stores often generate negative reactions in children because it signals the end of summer and the beginning of the school year. Even if your child enjoys school, it is difficult to let go of the carefree atmosphere of summer vacation. It is natural for a child to be resistant to the start of a school year. Yet, you have a significant role in helping your child to prepare mentally for that first day of school and for each school day afterwards. Your child's success in school is driven by attitude. If your child has a positive attitude towards school, then he or she will have a better chance for success. If your child dreads attending school, then achieving success will be more of a challenge. You can help create a positive attitude in your child towards school, and, consequently, prepare him or her for success.

The first step in shaping your child's attitude about school is to reflect on your own attitude. If you had a positive and enjoyable experience as a student in school, you will probably communicate this upbeat attitude to your child through your words and actions. Your child's perceptions about school will be filtered through your experience, and he or she will absorb your enthusiasm towards school. Children take cues from their parents on how to feel about something. So, if you enjoyed school, your child will likely have the expectation that school is a good place. Ideally, we like to think that school was a good place for everyone, but many parents had difficult times in school. You may have struggled academically and barely graduated or even dropped out of school before graduation. You may have enjoyed learning, but you had a bad experience with a teacher that tainted your perception of school. School may also have been a difficult place for you because of the actions of other students who teased, bullied, harassed or ignored you.

> *Carol hated school. She was always overweight, and the other kids called her names and made fun of her every day. Even though her daughter is not overweight, Carol worries constantly that her daughter might be teased. She does not want her daughter to be humiliated and embarrassed like she was. So, she is thinking about home-schooling her daughter.*

Experiences such as this will leave a bitter memory for any one about school, but every child will have a different experience. It is difficult not worry that your child will struggle in the same ways that you did, but you must separate your memories from your child's experience. Your child will not benefit from you having a negative attitude about going to school. Your child will look to you to decide how he or she should feel about school. If you had a challenging time in school, you can acknowledge to yourself that school was a difficult place for you. Yet, allow your child the opportunity to develop his or her own experience of school.

You can help your child develop a positive attitude towards school. Spend time with your child discussing what to expect in the school day. Discuss the daily activities such as reading, art, recess, and lunch. Many children fear getting lost in the "big" school building, riding the bus, making friends or having a mean teacher. Take your child to tour the school before his or her first day so your child is more familiar with the school layout. When you visit the school, show your child that you are excited for him or her. Teach your child—through your attitude—that going to school is a great adventure. Write down information that your child needs to remember such as locker number, room number, and the teacher's name. Contact the school, and ask if your child can meet the teacher beforehand to alleviate fears of a mean teacher. If your child is a new student, contact the school and request a buddy for him or her who will show your child around the first day and eat lunch with him or her. When school begins, leave notes for your child in his or her lunch reminding your child that you are thinking of him or her during the day. Create a routine for after school where your child can share about the day with you. Show interest in what your child is learning in school. Let your child know that his or her school experience is important to you.

Younger children can have anxiety about the every day routines involved in going to school. Restroom breaks can cause worry for younger children as they worry that they might have an accident before a break, or they might fear the actual school restroom. Talk to your child about his or her fears, and enlist the help of the teacher for support if necessary. Young children might still want to suck their thumb in school or bring a comforting stuffed animal. These children can be targets for teasing, so work with your child before school begins to lessen the thumb sucking or attachment to an object. You can give your child a smaller object to keep in his or her pocket for comfort if he or she needs to have something concrete to hold during the day. Anxiety, though, can strike at any age.

Dad: Adolph, it is time to get up and get ready for school.

Adolph: Dad, my stomach hurts. I need to stay home.

Dad: Adolph, you have told me all week that your stomach hurts, and you have not been to school. We saw the doctor yesterday, and she said you are fine. You cannot stay home from school another day.

Adolph: Dad, I can't go to school if I am sick. I NEED to stay home.

Dad: Adolph, I know you are having a tough time being the new student in school. That would be hard for anyone. But, if you don't go to school, you won't make any friends. I will go with you this morning and talk to your counselor. I will ask her to find you someone in your classes who you can talk to and eat lunch with. Once you make friends, you will enjoy school. I will help you with this.

Children of all ages can have intense anxiety about going to school. They fear being away from home and their family, or they fear not knowing what to expect from school. This often occurs at the start of elementary or middle school, or it can occur after a child has spent an extended period of time at home, i.e.: summer vacation or holiday breaks. Anxiety about going to school can also appear after a stressful event in a child's life such as a death in the family or a change in schools. A child who is anxious about going to school might complain of a headache or stomachache before school. These symptoms usually disappear if the child is allowed to stay at home, and they will surface again the next morning. The longer a child is allowed to stay at home, the more difficult it will be for him or her to go to school. Discuss your child's fears with him or her, and be empathetic with your child. Yet, do not allow your child to stay at home because he or she is anxious about attending school. Take your child to school and meet with the counselor. Inform the counselor of your child's anxiety, and ask for help in making the transition from home to school a successful one. Keep your goodbyes short in the morning, and then allow the teacher to provide a distracting activity for your child when you leave. A child is often fine once he or she gets to school. The anxiety is related more to leaving the house or leaving you. If your child is young, talk with the teacher about you staying for a portion of the day to ease the transition. If your child continues to have anxiety about attending school despite these strategies, consult with your health care provider or consult with the school counselor for assistance. Your child might have another issue that needs to be addressed before he or she can feel comfortable leaving you. Most children's anxieties, though, can be alleviated with a few interventions.

Be positive about the benefits and joys of going to school. Teach your child that receiving an education is the best tool available for success. Speak with confidence about making friends and having fun at school. Think of good memories that you have about school—even if they were simply eating lunch with friends each day—and share these with your child. You need to be your child's cheerleader when it comes to preparing him or her for school. If you remain positive and optimistic about going to school, your child will have a better chance for success.

4

Actively Monitor Your Child's Academic Progress

Ms. Johnson: I want to know why my daughter failed! My daughter is smart, and she has never failed. Why did this happen!

Teacher: Ms. Johnson, your daughter's report card was mailed home every six weeks during the school year which showed her failing grades. Additionally, I called you several times and left messages, and I sent you letters asking you to meet with me regarding your daughter. You never responded. Your daughter can go to summer school to make up her grades, but we need to meet with you to set up a plan to help your daughter be successful next year.

I get at least one of these phone calls every June from parents who are surprised that their child failed the school year. These parents, typically, have not monitored their child's progress throughout the school year, so they are surprised when their child fails. Children spend close to 200 days a year in school, and many parents do not pay attention to how their child is doing in school until they receive the final report card. It is too late to help your child be successful in school if you wait until you receive the final grades. Your child needs for you to be involved and informed about his or her academics from the first day of school.

A common mistake parents make is to not talk daily with their children about school. A typical conversation between a parent and child sounds like this:

Dad: How was your day?

Nadia: Fine.

Dad: What did you do?

Nadia: Nothing.

Dad: Okay. Great.

(Dad turns the radio on.)

Children do not spend an entire day in school and do "nothing." Something happens—many things happen—in school each day, and it is a parent's role to know what his or her child did. Ask specific, open-ended questions when talking to your child about school. Open-ended questions require a more detailed response other than, "yes" or "no." Open-ended questions begin with how, why, what or even tell me about… If you ask about a specific class or course, it helps your child focus his or her answer. These questions can include:

"What did you do in math today?"

"Tell me about your presentation in history."

"Why did you make a C on your science test? What three things can you do differently next time to earn a better grade?"

"How did you spend your recess time today?"

Get into the habit of visiting with your child each day to discuss school. Learn when is the best time to talk to your child about his or her day. Some children are ready to talk as soon as they see their parents, and others need time to unwind. Establish an afternoon or evening ritual for when you will discuss your child's day, and ask specific, open-ended questions about classes. This will keep you more informed about what you child is doing in school.

ASSIGNMENT SHEETS

Actively monitor your child's grades. Many schools have started using assignment sheets, assignment notebooks, or student planners where students write down what they did in class each day; they record their homework assignments; and teachers can make comments or write down students' current grades. This will help you keep abreast of your child's grades as well as know what homework needs to be completed each evening. If your school does not have such a system in place, ask your child's teacher to work with you on using assignment sheets or notebooks. These are a great way to communicate daily with your child's teacher, and it will help your child be better organized.

HOMEWORK

Students frequently fail classes because they do not do homework. As a rule of thumb, children should spend ten minutes per grade level per day on homework. For example, a child in sixth grade should spend about sixty minutes (6 x 10) a day on homework. Check your child's assignment sheet or student planner to see what homework needs to be completed. After your child has finished the homework, check it to make sure it is complete, and ask your child what he or she did for each subject. You do not have to make sure that the homework is done correctly; you just want to be sure it is complete. Once your child has proven to be dependable in completing homework, you can check the homework less often. Yet, keep monitoring your child's grades to ensure that he or she continues to be successful with academics.

It is often tempting for parents to be overly helpful with their child's homework, and some parents end up doing the work themselves. Your child is given homework to practice a skill or extend a lesson. If you do your child's homework for him or her, it robs your child of the opportunity to learn. You can help your child be successful with homework by ensuring that he or she has a regular routine for doing homework, i.e.: completing homework as soon as he or she comes home from school or immediately after dinner. Do not allow your child to wait until before bedtime to complete homework, as it will be rushed and probably incomplete. Your child also needs a regular place to study at home. It can be a desk or the kitchen table, but it should be stocked with paper, pencils, pens, a dictionary, and other needed supplies. Younger siblings should be taught not to disturb your child when he or she is studying. Lastly, the television should be turned off during homework time--no exceptions. If your child does not have homework, he or she should spend the homework time reading a book. This will help keep the homework routine consistent as well as improve reading skills. There are many websites designed to help students with study and research skills including:

www.discoveryschool.com

www.factmonster.com

www.nationalgeographic.org

www.yahooligans.com.

Consult with your child's teacher or school counselor to learn about additional resources.

PARENT/TEACHER CONFERENCES

You can establish communication with your child's teacher through the assignment sheet or notebook. It is also important to talk to your child's teacher on the telephone, through email or meet in person at least once during the first few months of school. You do not have to wait until your child is having a problem before talking to the teacher. You can establish a strong relationship with your child's teacher by asking about the teacher's program, discussing your expectations, and sharing information about your child that might be helpful for the teacher to know. You are a partner with the teacher in your child's education. If you establish a working relationship with the teacher in the beginning of the school year, this will help your child be more successful in the classroom.

When your child is having problems and you set up a meeting

with your child's teacher, be prepared. Talk to your child about the class and find out your child's perceptions about his or her progress. Ask your child in what areas he or she is excelling, what areas need improvement, and if there is anything that he or she would like for you to discuss with the teacher. Make notes for yourself to take to the meeting about what you want to share with the teacher and what questions you want to ask. Be on time for the conference, and do not stay past the time given for the meeting. Teachers generally meet with parents during their conference periods, and they cannot stay late for a meeting since they have to return to class. Listen to what the teacher has to share about your child's progress--both academically and behaviorally. Ask the teacher if he or she has any concerns about how your child is doing. If your child is not making satisfactory progress, ask the teacher for specific suggestions on how to help your child improve. This is the most important part of the meeting as it is the information you need to help your child be successful. Do not be afraid to ask for clarification if you do not understand something the teacher is telling you. End the meeting by summarizing the decisions you made together with the teacher, and establish when you should follow-up for a progress report. The relationship you build with your child's teacher will be another useful tool in helping your child succeed in school.

ADDITIONAL SUPPORT

Despite a parent's best efforts, some children have difficulties learning.

Sara's dad is frustrated. Sara has always taken longer to understand her schoolwork, but it seems to be getting more difficult. She is spending two hours a night on homework, and she goes to a tutor twice a week. She is only in the fifth grade. What is it going to be like in high school? Why is she having so much trouble?

If your child is struggling in school, it does not mean that you are a failure as a parent; it means simply that your child needs additional support to be successful. The reasons for learning difficulties vary from genetics to environment. All children, though, need to be given the best opportunity to be successful. If your child is struggling in the classroom with either behavior or academics, meet with your child's teacher to discuss what interventions can be used to help your child be successful. If these strategies are not effective, ask your child's teacher or counselor what testing is available to assess your child's abilities. These tests will give better information on what your child's strengths and weaknesses are, and it will show if more intervention is needed. Many parents are resistant to testing because they do not want their child to be "labeled." So many students these days are receiving additional help in a variety of areas that receiving extra help no longer has the stigma it used to have. I have seen students struggle in school because their parents believed that their children were just lazy. Students who struggle in school on a daily basis are more likely to hate school, get into trouble, develop symptoms of depression, and/or eventually drop out. There are numerous programs designed to help students be successful. Do not deny your child the opportunities for success because of your own fears. If your child is not doing well and you have tried several strategies to help him or her, talk to your child's school counselor about testing. Your counselor will be able to discuss the options with you that will help your child find success.

Some children are not successful in school because they struggle with Attention Deficit Hyperactivity Disorder—ADHD. Symptoms of ADHD can include inattentiveness, careless mistakes, inability to listen and/or follow directions, unable to finish tasks, losing things, easily distracted, being disorganized, and unable to sit still. All children can demonstrate these behaviors at some point, but when the behaviors are persistent it could indicate a need for an evaluation by your health care provider. Children with ADHD struggle to be successful, and without intervention, these children are at-risk for academic failure, social isolation, and depression. Your health care provider can help you determine if you child needs interventions and what appropriate actions can be taken to help your child succeed. Several websites are available to help parents learn more about learning disabilities and working with children with special learning needs. Some of these websites are:

The Learning Disabilities Association of America at www.ldaamerica.org

LD on-line at www.ldonline.org

The National Dissemination Center for Children with Disabilities at www.nichcy.org

Schwab Learning at www.schwablearning.org.

Your child's teacher or school counselor can provide you with additional resources to give you more information about meeting your child's learning needs.

You are the major force behind your child being successful in academics. You must be actively involved in your child's education for your child to be successful. When you establish high expectations for your child's learning, your child will rise to the expectation. Your partnership with your child's school is one of the most important relationships you can have for your child. Let your child know through your words and actions that you care about his or her progress and that you will be a part of his or her learning every day.

5

Teach Appropriate Ways to Interact with Others

Malcolm is in trouble again. He is waiting to see the vice principal because he punched another student. "I couldn't help it," Malcolm tells himself. "That kid deserved it for making fun of me, and my dad always tells me to defend myself. I shouldn't get in trouble for defending myself."

Malcolm is like many students in school. He did what his father taught him to do when having a conflict, but his actions caused him to be in trouble. Parents will often tell children to defend themselves if someone is bothering them. This advice causes problems for children because fighting is never acceptable in school, and children use this "permission to fight" as an excuse to handle their verbal and physical conflicts. I was standing in line at the grocery store one afternoon. The lady in the line next to me was speaking to a friend, and she said, "There is some girl pestering my son at school. I am so sick of it. I told him to just haul off and hit her if she keeps bothering him. I told him I would come to school and get him if he got in trouble for hitting the girl." Children become confused when they are behaving according to their parents' teachings and this behavior causes them to be disciplined at school. Children look to their parents to learn how to interact with others.

Your child learns how to interact with others by your teachings and observing your interactions with people. From the time children are babies, they observe how their parents respond to various situations, and they learn from their observations. If your child sees you yell at a store clerk because you are unhappy with the service, your child learns that yelling at people in public is acceptable. This could lead to your child yelling at students or teachers in school, and this is never acceptable. If your child observes you getting into a fistfight with a neighbor over a disagreement, your child learns that fighting is the way to resolve conflicts. This will carry over into the school setting as well, and your child will be punished for fighting. If your child experiences you calling him or her names when you get angry, your child learns that the appropriate way to respond when angry at someone is to call that person names. This will cause problems in the school when a child calls another student or a teacher a derogatory name. Conversely, if your child sees you treat others with respect and politeness, even when you are angry, he or she will learn the appropriate behaviors that are needed to be successful in school and society. Children learn how to behave and interact with people from their parents. Your role is to teach your child how to treat others with respect and consideration.

ANGER

James: Why are you so tired?

Heather: I couldn't sleep last night.

James: Why?

Heather: My parents were fighting again. They were yelling at each other all night. My little brother got scared, and he came into my room to sleep with me. I couldn't go to sleep.

James: When did they stop yelling?

Heather: The neighbors called the police at some point. When the police showed up, my parents quit yelling. But, I only slept a few hours after that.

There will be many times when your child is angry with another person. Anger is a normal part of being human. Yet, the ways that people choose to express anger can either resolve the conflict or escalate the problem. Children learn how to express anger from watching their parents. Children have trouble when they do not know how to express their anger or resolve conflicts appropriately. Parents must teach their children how to manage anger and resolve conflicts peacefully through their words and actions. Anger management skills include:

- recognizing how the body changes when a person gets angry, i.e.: breathing becomes rapid, muscles tense, face feels hot;
- knowing the signals the body sends when it is angry and immediately slowing down breathing to a steady pace;
- stepping back from the situation or person that is causing the anger;
- focusing on relaxing muscles by unclenching fists and relaxing jaw muscles; and
- counting backwards from ten to one.

Once a person has calmed down, he or she can work to resolve the conflict peacefully with the other person. If a compromise cannot be reached, the person can ask an objective third party to mediate a compromise. The school's counselor, administration or peer mediation program can assist in resolving many student conflicts. Students or parents may contact the school for assistance in resolving conflicts. Additionally, many schools teach anger management skills and conflict resolution. If your child needs to improve skills in these areas, contact your child's school counselor to learn about available resources. Your child needs to learn how to peacefully resolve conflicts for success in school and for his or her own safety in the community.

ACCEPTABLE BEHAVIOR

Teacher: Carlos, I need for you to throw away your lunch tray.

(Carlos ignores the teacher.)

Teacher: Carlos, please follow my directions and throw away your lunch tray.

Carlos: I'm not going to throw it away. It's not even mine.

Teacher: Carlos, I am not going to argue with you. I expect you to throw away your lunch tray.

Carlos: Man, you can't tell me what to do. I'll do what I want.

Learning how to follow directions and rules is a necessary skill for student success. Schools are designed to educate students in academics as well as prepare them for success in society. When a student graduates from high school, he or she should be able to follow the rules of society and live a responsible and successful life. The rules of schools often mirror the rules of society so that children learn society's expectations for its citizens. When the teachings of parents differ from the teachings of school, students are caught in the middle and left feeling confused.

You have your own philosophies about what is acceptable behavior and how to interact with other people. Yet, your philosophies may conflict with what is acceptable behavior at a school. Most schools have a student handbook that outlines the rules and expectations of students. Review this handbook with your child, and be sure that he or she understands the information. You may not agree with all of the information in the handbook, but it does outline the school's expectations of their students, and your child will get into trouble if he or she does not follow the rules. If you disagree with the school's rules, share your complaints with the principal or school board. Do not put your child in the middle of your conflict with the school by encouraging him or her to break the rules because you do not agree with them. Your child should follow the rules until you are able to come to an agreement with the school regarding your concerns.

Your child will have an easier time achieving success in school if he or she understands appropriate manners. Children need to know how to respectfully speak to adults, how to accept "No" for an answer, how to say "please" and "thank you" and other forms of manners. The book *The Essential 55* by Ron Clark will give you further information about how to teach manners to your child so that he or she will be more successful. School officials appreciate when students are able to demonstrate courtesy and respect towards them and other students.

A child's ability to achieve success in school is largely dependent on how well he or she interacts with others. A child may be very intelligent, but if he or she spends a lot of time out of the classroom and in the office for inappropriate behavior, it will be difficult to maintain passing grades. Your child will learn from you how to behave appropriately, and this will help guide him or her towards success.

6

Allow Your Child to Experience Consequences in School

Mrs. Clover: I can't believe you called me from work for this. Henry didn't do anything. The other kids were fighting. Henry was just standing there. It is not his fault if someone pushed him into the fight.

Vice-Principal: Ms. Clover, two teachers saw Henry go up to another student and punch him in the face. Henry is the one that started the fight.

Mrs. Clover: Well that other kid must have done something to provoke the fight. Henry would not just go hit a kid. Is the other kid being punished?

"It's not my child's fault! My child didn't do anything!" These exclamations are made to me every year when children get into trouble. Some parents have a hard time accepting that their children are responsible for misbehavior, and they are quick to make excuses for their children while blaming the school or someone else. These parents are refusing to allow their children to accept responsibility for their choices. They believe they are helping their children by rescuing them from consequences. These parents are just like many other parents. They believe that they are protecting their children out of love when, in fact, they are not allowing their children to learn from their mistakes. This rescuing will create barriers to success for their children.

Making bad choices and facing consequences is a normal part of childhood. Children learn how to be responsible, make good choices, and develop a healthy self-esteem from experiencing consequences. Every bad decision and ensuing consequence is a learning opportunity for children. They learn that making a certain choice will lead them to an undesirable consequence. This lesson guides them to making a different choice the next time. If parents rescue their children from experiencing consequences, the children are never allowed the chance to grow. The opportunity to strengthen their character and learn that they can make good decisions in the future is taken away. Children who do not learn from their mistakes will continue to make more mistakes. Eventually, a child's education is affected because more time is spent in the office being disciplined than in the classroom learning.

Children will get in trouble in school. It might be a minor situation like being tardy to class, or it might be a major offense involving drugs. These are the times that children can learn about taking responsibility for their actions. If your child gets in trouble at school, do not rescue him or her. Discuss the situation with your child; support the consequences given by the school; and help him or her think of ways to do things differently next time.

Debbie: They said I was tardy six times this month, and now I am suspended from pep squad. It isn't fair because other girls have been tardy, but they weren't suspended.

Mom: Did you know that you could be suspended if you were tardy?

Debbie: Yeah, but no one ever pays attention to those rules. Can't you call the sponsor, Mom, and get me off of suspension?

Mom: I'm sorry honey, I can't. You knew the consequences of being tardy, but you choose to be tardy anyway. I know it is disappointing to be suspended—especially right before the Homecoming game. But, let's talk about what you can do from now on so that you are not tardy to class.

If your child gets into trouble, empathize with your child about his or her feelings towards the incident, but do not try to fix it. You can let your child know that you are disappointed in the choices made and you still love and support him or her. Be careful, though, to not berate your child for what happened. Let your child know that he or she has to accept responsibility for actions and experience consequences, and that you trust that a better choice will be made next time. If your child is suspended from school because of behavior, make his or her time at home a challenging one. Do not allow your child to watch television or sleep late. Assign your child chores around the house and set aside time for him or her to study and read. Occupy every moment of your child's day with tasks. One parent of a suspended child had his son move a pile of rocks from one end of the backyard to another and then back again. Children who are suspended from school should learn that being in school is preferable to staying at home.

Some children have physical or emotional problems that contribute to their difficult behavior. If your child is constantly getting into trouble in school, talk with your child's teacher and counselor. Listen to their observations about what might be causing your child's problems. Work with the school to establish a behavior plan for your child. If your child continues to misbehave despite interventions, seek professional help. Your school counselor can provide you with resources for assistance. Children do not like to get into trouble. Children who can control their behavior but choose to misbehave are often seeking attention. A professional counselor can work with your child to learn more accepting ways of getting his or her needs met. A child who cannot control his or her behavior may need a combination of counseling and medication. Children who frequently get into trouble can become depressed and frustrated. Their learning is affected, and they often do not have friends. They are at a higher risk for having more severe problems as adults. These children need help to feel better about themselves and to learn how to control their emotions. Do not feel embarrassed or ashamed about your child needing help. The right services can help your child find hope and success.

Allowing your child the chance to grow from his or her mistakes will help your child achieve success in school. Your child will learn responsibility and how to make better decisions. One of the most important jobs of parents is to guide their children as they learn how to manage their behavior. Your child will have a better opportunity to mature into a successful adult when you resist the desire to rescue him or her from consequences given by the school and allow your child the room to learn from mistakes.

7

Be Involved in Career Preparation

Ellen: Grandma, I want to be a computer animator when I grow up.

Grandma: Honey, I have no idea what that is.

Ellen: It's kind of like drawing on the computer.

Grandma: You can't make money doing that. You should be a nurse or something that is stable.

Ellen: No, Grandma. I want to work with computers. Come on and I'll show you what I can do.

My mother went to college to become an elementary school teacher. She told me that women in the 1950's had two approved choices for a college degree: nursing or teaching. She chose teaching. Many people, men and women, did not choose to attend college in the 1950's. Women were encouraged to get married, stay home and raise a family. Men had the option of going to college. If, though, they wanted to get a job right out of high school, they could find good-paying jobs in which to settle. Our society has changed since the 1950's. Women can no longer count on men to support them, and men struggle to support a family with a job that only requires a high school degree. Schools have changed as well reflecting the trends of society, and much time is spent from elementary to high school preparing students for a career.

One of the purposes of school is to prepare children to be successful and contributing members of society. This includes helping students discover what career path they want to follow. Careers have changed over the years, and there are many opportunities available for students today that did not exist twenty years ago. The field of technology, for example, has created thousands of well-paying careers that are attractive to today's youth. Parents often are not aware of the many careers available today, so they might discourage their children from following a different path than the one with which they are familiar. One of the challenges of today's parents is to be open to the numerous opportunities available for today's children. Schools will work with students to help them explore career options, but parents should be actively involved with this process as well.

Talk to your child about what is interesting to him or her and what careers could be related to his or her interests. Start talking to your child at a young age about possible careers. This will send your child the message that you expect your child to graduate from school and find an interesting job that he or she will enjoy. A child who has a career goal in mind is more likely to stay motivated to do well in school. A child's interest is a great indicator to what he or she might want to pursue in a career. A student may change his or her mind about a career many times while growing up, and this is normal. As students learn more about the opportunities available to them, and as they grow and change, their interests will change. Schools generally provide interests inventory tests for students to help them focus on their interests. The Occupational Outlook Handbook found in the library or on the Internet provides a listing of numerous career fields and the degrees required to work in those fields. Additionally, your school counselor can give you information about what career development programs are available in your child's school.

Students today are being encouraged to obtain a higher education beyond high school. A degree or certification beyond a high school diploma will open up many more doors for students. Students who graduate from high school and continue with their education will be qualified to get better jobs, earn more money, and acquire a wide range of knowledge in a variety of subjects. Students who are not interested in attending a four-year college can benefit from the skills and knowledge obtained by attending a two-year community college for a degree or certification in an area of specialty. Students of parents who did not attend college are less likely to seek an education beyond high school. According to a recent study, 82 percent of students whose parents graduated from college enrolled in a college immediately after finishing high school. Yet, only 54 percent of students whose parents did not attend college enrolled in college, and if the parents did not graduate from high school, the number drops to 36 percent. (U.S. Department of Education, 2001) If you did not go to school beyond high school, the prospect of your child leaving home, going to a college campus, and paying for the education can be overwhelming.

Linda: Dad, some people came to school today to talk to us about college. They said that I could get money to pay for college. I really want to go. I really want to be a doctor.

Dad: No, Linda. We have talked about this before. I do not want you going away to college. Your place is here at home. Your mother and I did not going to college; your brothers did not go to college. We are doing fine, and you will too.

Linda: Dad, one of the things they told us is that it can be scary for our parents to allow us to go to college if our parents did not go. I know you are happy with your life, but this is my life. College is a good thing, and being a doctor is something I always wanted to do. At least come to school and talk to my counselor about it. This is important to me.

Dad: Okay, I am still not sure about this. But, I will listen to what your counselor has to say.

The unknown is frightening. For many parents, higher education is an unknown, and it is easier to forbid their children from pursuing their education beyond high school rather than venture into unfamiliar territory. Even parents who went to college can be overwhelmed by the changes that have occurred since they attended school. Yet, you do not have to do this alone. Ask you child's school counselor for information about preparing your child for a higher education. Programs are being implemented in the elementary, middle and high school levels to encourage students to pursue an education beyond high school. Your child's school counselor will be able to provide you with the information that is appropriate for your child's age. Paying for a higher education can be a big deterrent for parents, yet there are many financial aid programs available for students who want to continue school beyond high school regardless of income level. Financial aid includes money given to students to pay for education expenses, and money loaned to students and parents at a low interest for education costs. More information about financial aid opportunities can be found at the Federal Student Aid Information Center www.studentaid.ed.gov or 1-800-433-3234. Another source is the National Center for Education Statistics' College Opportunities on-line at www.nces.ed.gov/ipeds.cool/. Information on available college scholarships can be found at www.collegeanswer.com and www.collegeboard.com.

Children often follow in their parents' career paths because they do not know what other options are open to them, or they are discouraged from trying something different from their parents. Part of your child's success in school depends on whether or not he or she is interested in what is being taught. When your child gets excited about the possibilities of an education, then he or she will more likely be successful. It can be frightening for your child to choose a different path than you did, but it is important for his or her success to have many available options. Encourage your child to explore all of the career opportunities available, and talk to your child about his or her interests. Set your standards high for your child's education, and let him or her know that your expectation is that he or she will attend school beyond high school for a degree or certificate. Do not let fear of the unknown limit your child. Career possibilities are endless, and your child's success in school is influenced by his or her ability to explore all options.

8

Instill Good Sleep Habits

Thomas is in the counselor's office for falling asleep in class. His teacher had been trying to work with him since the school year started to help Thomas stay awake. But, he continues to fall asleep despite her efforts.

Counselor: Thomas, why do you think you are falling asleep during school?

Thomas: I don't know. I am just tired.

Counselor: What time to you go to bed at night.

Thomas: Usually around 1:00.

Counselor: And, what time to you get up.

Thomas: My mom wakes me up at 7:30.

Counselor: Do you get out of bed as soon as she wakes you up?

Thomas: No, she usually has to come in a lot until I wake up. When she starts yelling, I know I have to get up.

Counselor: So you are getting about six and one-half hours of sleep each night. You need at least eight to eleven hours of sleep each night so you will be more alert during the day. Why do you stay up so late?

Thomas: I don't know. I am usually watching T.V., and I don't want to go to bed.

Counselor: Does your mother have a set bedtime for you?

Thomas: Yeah. She tells me to go to bed by 10:00, but she is usually asleep before then, so I just stay up as late as I want.

Thomas' situation is not unusual. Bedtimes are not as structured for children as they used to be. Families are becoming busier, and they are trying to fit more activities into the day. Consequently, children are being allowed to stay up later at night to complete homework, wind-down from the day, or because their parents are tired and they go to bed before their children. It is vital to children's health and academic success that they get enough sleep each night. Children are falling asleep in class or they are unable to focus because they are so tired. The effects of lack of sleep are inattention in school, poor grades, illness, depression, caffeine dependence, and for teenagers, auto accidents. Lack of sleep will affect your child's overall well being, and it is a problem that requires attention.

Your child should be getting between eight to eleven hours of sleep each night. If this is not happening, then your child's schedule needs to be adjusted to allow him or her to go to bed at a reasonable hour. This might mean reducing the number of after-school activities in which your child is involved. If your child cannot complete homework each night before a reasonable hour because he or she is getting home too late from other activities, including an after-school job, then he or she is over-involved. Children are children. Their days do not need to be scheduled to capacity with extra-curricular activities and social events during the school year. They need to have some relaxing time in the evening, and they need to be able to go to bed at a reasonable hour. Discuss with your child his or her schedule. If your child is not getting enough sleep because of other activities, help your child determine which activities to give up so that he or she is not sleep-deprived.

Some children may be staying up too late because of the amount of time they spend working on homework. If your child is going to bed late because he or she is spending too much time each night on homework, then the class load needs to be evaluated. Children who take several honors or advanced classes often find themselves overwhelmed with the amount of work required to fulfill the course requirements. You should consider reducing the amount of these classes your child is taking if the homework is too time-consuming. If your child is in all regular classes and he or she is still spending a lot of time on homework each night, then talk with the teachers or counselor to see if your child might need outside assistance with learning the material.

Some children are overburdened with daily household chores or babysitting duties, which prevent them from getting adequate sleep. It is important for children to have responsibilities around the house, but these responsibilities should not be so time consuming that they make it difficult for your child to complete homework and lead a balanced life. If your child is spending too much time helping with household responsibilities, make some adjustments in chores so that he or she will have time for homework, activities and rest.

Many parents would be surprised to learn that even through their children are in bed at least eight hours each night; they are still struggling with daytime sleepiness. Numerous factors can prevent children from getting a good night's sleep and feeling rested during the day.

- Children who are overly stressed or worried about an issue—whether it is their own problem or a family member's or friend's problem—will have trouble sleeping during the night. Their thoughts and worries prevent them from relaxing enough to fall into a deep sleep.
- Children who do not feel safe in their homes and/or neighborhoods will find it difficult to sleep well at night. They feel they must stay awake to protect themselves and/or their families from harm.
- Vision problems can lead to daytime sleepiness. Children who have difficulty seeing classroom boards or reading texts because of eye strain can struggle to stay awake during class.
- Medication—prescription and over-the-counter—can cause children to be sleepy during the day.

- Children who abuse drugs often have a difficult time staying awake during the day. (More information about substance abuse can be found in Lesson 21: Know the Signs of Alcohol and Drug Abuse.)
- Daytime sleepiness can also result when the classroom material is too easy or too difficult.

Talk to your child about his or her sleep problems if your child is unable to sleep well during the night and/or struggles with daytime sleepiness. If you are unable to resolve the problem, consult with your child's teacher, school counselor, school nurse and/or health care provider. Your child needs adequate sleep in order to function well during the day and be successful. Consultation with a professional might be needed to solve your child's sleep-related problem.

Children should have the time each day to attend school, participate in an enjoyable activity, complete homework and relax. As a parent, your role is to ensure that your child is able to do these things each day without sacrificing sleep. Establishing a bedtime routine when children are young— which can include a winding-down period, a final activity of the day such as reading or visiting, and a set bedtime—will help instill good sleep habits. You might meet with some resistance from your child if you decide that he or she needs to give up an activity in order to have a more balanced life, but your child's health and academic success depend on it.

9

Plan for Summer Activities

Counselor: What did you do over the summer, Bobby?

Bobby: Nothing.

Counselor: Really! You did nothing all day.

Bobby: Yeah.

Counselor: You did not go on a trip; go to the movies; go swimming?

Bobby: Nah.

Counselor: Are you saying you just sat in a chair all summer?

Bobby: (smiling) Yeah.

Counselor: Well, I hope it was a comfortable chair.

It is surprising how many students tell me they did "nothing" all summer. Although children do things all summer, for many children, they do nothing that is worth sharing. These children spend their summer watching television, sleeping and hanging-out with friends. Summer is a time for children to relax and have a break from studies, but it also needs to be a time that is productive as well.

FAMILY TIME

Summer is an excellent time for families to build stronger relationships. The school year is a busy time, and family time can be limited. Summer is the time when families can be together to travel, go to the park, or play games at home. This may require you to take some days off from work, but they will be days well spent. The times you spend with your child during the summer are powerful memory builders. When people recall childhood memories, they usually involve activities they did with their families. The experience of spending time with our family activates all of our senses, and stronger memories are created. Family vacations provide opportunities for families to eat every meal together, sleep in close quarters, play games, share stories, and strengthen relationships. Family vacations renew the bond of the family, and they remind children of the support and love that is shared with family members. Use family vacations as a time to talk to your child about a variety of topics. When you are traveling in the car, turn off the DVDs or videos and talk. Your connection with your child will be strengthened with every meaningful conversation. Children who have enjoyable experiences with their families during the summer are usually better prepared to commit to another year of learning when the school year begins. For more ideas on family time, visit www.puttingfamilyfirst.org.

PARTICIPATE IN ACTIVITIES

Summer can also be a time for children to become involved in an organization that offers summer activities or camps. Children can explore potential career areas by participating in summer activities, or they can learn new skills that might help them in the future. Organizations and churches offer activities and camps open to children of all ages. Contact your school or church for suggestions of organizations that offer classes, camps and activities during the summer. Your child's involvement in activities during the summer can create exciting learning opportunities.

Help your child find something that he or she enjoys. If your child does not feel that he or she is good at anything, summer is an excellent time for your child to discover something that he or she can do well. Summer is a great time to learn a new hobby or sport such as karate. If you child is old enough, he or she might also want to consider getting a summer job. This will keep your child active, provide money for savings and fun, and give him or her the opportunity to meet other people outside of school. There is no reason for children to spend their summer watching television all day or spending all day hanging out with their friends at the mall. It is fine to do these activities during the summer, but if your child's whole summer consists of watching television or hanging out with friends, he or she is missing some exciting learning opportunities.

READING

Reading should be an essential part of your child's summer. Your child should spend some time each day reading for pleasure with the television turned off. This will improve your child's reading skills, as well as enhance brain activity. Poor reading skills contribute to school failure because students who do not read well have trouble in all subject areas. School failure increases the risk of becoming involved in risky behavior such as substance abuse and sexual activity. Strengthen your child's reading skills by setting a goal for your child to read at least thirty minutes each day. If your child is younger, read a story together. Discuss what you are reading, and have your child summarize the story. If your child is older, you can either read the same book or just read at the same time. Ask your child about what he or she is reading, and let him or her tell you about the book's plot, characters, or topic. Send a message to your child that reading is important. Make reading a priority as a daily activity for both you and your child. The following tips will help encourage reading in your family.

- Agree on a family reading time where all members read at the same time each day.
- Read together outside in the backyard, at the park, or at the beach or lake.
- Start a family or neighborhood book club, and have each person read the same book to discuss together.

- Go the library as a family and check out books.
- Go to book readings at your local bookstore.
- Give your child a subscription to his or her favorite magazine.
- Provide your child with a dictionary, and encourage him or her to look up unfamiliar words.
- Give books as gifts.

Make reading an essential part of your child's summertime routine to help facilitate success for your child.

Summer is a time for kids to relax and enjoy a break from the demands of school. Yet, it should not be a time where students "do nothing" all day, every day. Balance your child's summer with family activities, participation in a summer program, reading, and relaxing. This will provide your child with many learning opportunities and good memories while preparing him or her for another successful school year.

10

Teach Responsibility

Barbara has reached her limit. She has three teenaged sons at home, and all she does is pick-up after them and clean. They refuse to keep their rooms neat, and they will not help with simple chores around the house. She thought she was doing them a favor by not giving them responsibilities around the house so they could have more time for fun, but now she sees that decision as a mistake. She wonders how they are going to make it in life if they can't even take out the trash.

A major job in parenting is to teach children responsibility both with tasks and money. Many children encounter problems in school because they are accustomed to someone meeting all of their needs at home. They are surprised when they are required to throw away their own lunch tray at school, or they have to clean a desk on which they made stray marks. These little lessons in responsibility are building character in children, and they are preparing them for a successful life.

Children can start learning responsibility at a young age. They can be taught to pick up their toys when they are toddlers, and children can be given simple chores to do around the house when they are school-aged. Children need to learn that the world does not exist to meet their needs. Children exist to create a better world. When children experience having responsibilities at home, they are able to transfer this learning to the school setting. This will help them be more successful in school as teachers know they can depend on the responsible children to help make the classroom a better place to learn. Children who show initiative in being responsible are given more opportunities and leadership roles that instill a healthier self-esteem and motivation to achieve. Children who grow-up to be society's leaders begin their training in school. They practice being leaders in the classroom, and they develop the skills needed to be successful. Children who learn that they are responsible for their own choices and lives are more likely to make healthier choices as adults and find greater success.

Children can also be taught responsibility with finances. Success in today's society requires knowledge about how to handle money responsibly. Building a savings and spending wisely are skills that are essential for thriving in today's economy. Children can be taught to save a portion of all of the money they are given from gifts, allowances, or earned through chores. This is money that should never be touched until they graduate from high school, and they can use the money for college or to get settled in a home. The remainder of the money children receive can be split between saving for big purchases like electronics or a bicycle, and fun money to spend on snacks or gifts.

Parents are the primary role models for children on how to responsibly handle money. If children see their parents saving money and spending money wisely, then they will be more likely to follow this example. Many adults find themselves in financial difficulties due to overspending and accumulating credit card debt. When children see their parents living outside of their financial limits and becoming overwhelmed with debt, children learn dangerous financial lessons about how to manage money. Additionally, the emotional stress that results from debt will cause a strain on the family's health and relationships. Children must learn that making financial choices based on an available line of credit is not a healthy plan for managing finances. Children become easy targets for credit card companies when they turn eighteen years old, and without the proper role modeling and education, they are likely to fall into a debt trap from which they cannot emerge. This financial burden and its accompanying emotional strain can be overwhelming. Parents have a responsibility to their children to follow healthy and reasonable financial plans and teach their children how to responsibly manage their own money. These financial lessons can dramatically change the economic future of adolescents. More information about living financially responsible can be found on Dave Ramsey's website www.daveramsey.com (which also has a special section for kids) and Suze Orman's website at www.suzeorman. com. Children can learn that being responsible with money can lead to a secure and successful life.

Children should also be taught to never lend money to friends. Students have no qualms about asking for money from other students. If a student is known at school for always having money, he or she will be the target of other students looking for money. The word "borrow" in school does not mean it will be returned. It simply means, "give away." Teach your child to not be taken advantage of by other students looking for someone to finance their lunch snacks.

Children can also be taught responsibility with their toys and possessions. Children need to know how to take care of their possessions and keep them in good condition. They need to know how to respect other people's property as well. Vandalism is a problem among school children, but you can teach your child to respect his or her own property and the property of others.

Teaching children to be responsible is not a lesson that can be taught in a short amount of time. It is a lesson that is taught daily throughout childhood. Children who are given responsibility at home gain a sense of importance in the family, and they feel needed by their families. Children who have chores at home learn persistence in accomplishing a task. Persistence is a skill that will help them achieve success. Parents are the main teachers of responsibility for children, and their lessons will resonate throughout their children's lives guiding them towards success.

11

Eat Dinner Together

The Patricks always eat dinner together. The kids are involved in various activities after school, but everyone knows that they are expected to be sitting at the dinner table at 6:00 every evening. This is the time that they can come together as a family and talk about their day. The kids complain about it sometimes because they are not ready to come home, and it is not always easy for the parents to leave their jobs either. But, the family is committed to spend this time together each day for each other.

Eating dinner together is a simple lesson in helping your child be successful. Families who eat dinner together are able to connect with each other at the end of the day and strengthen the family bond. Yet, eating dinner together can often be one of the most difficult strategies to implement. Families are busy. Children are busy with after school activities like band, athletics, clubs, and karate. Parents are busy with their jobs, volunteer activities, and errands. It is easy for everyone to become busy and never see each other. When families do not spend time together, the bond begins to weaken, and kids start falling through the cracks. Parents are not able to stay connected with their children, and they are less likely to know when their children are in trouble. Eating dinner with your child is an excellent way to strengthen the bond you have with your child.

Talk with your child during dinner. The television should be turned off, the telephone unanswered and the newspaper put aside. Do not use this time to talk to your spouse about adult topics. This is a time to include the whole family in the conversation. The conversation can begin with each person sharing something about his or her day, and it can broaden to other topics. This is not a time to lecture or discuss problems; save those discussions for after the meal. Dinner should be a relaxing time of good food and enjoyable conversation. Dinner conversation is an excellent time to teach and share your values with your child. This can be done with stories from your past or from your recent experiences. Children need to be guided in defining their values, and dinner is an excellent time to discuss what is important. If you are stuck on how to start a lively conversation, try one of these topics.

Conversation starters:

What was the best thing about your day?
What was the worst thing about your day?
Tell about a time when…
What is the best/worst thing about…
Describe your favorite meal.
What do you miss about last year?
What do you look forward to this year?

More ideas on good family dinner conversation can be found in the book *Keep Talking: Conversation Starters for the Family Meal* by M. Lahr and J. Pfitzinger. The website www.puttingfamilyfirst.org/html/dinner_time.html also gives additional ideas on creating enjoyable family dinners.

Family dinners do not have to be a daily event, but your child will benefit the more often you have them. The discussions do not have to begin and end at the dinner table. Preparing for the meal together and cleaning up together afterwards are also excellent moments to talk to your child. You can also have family breakfasts or lunches if dinners are too difficult to coordinate. Regardless of when you eat together, be sure that the meals are filled with laughter and good conversation.

Eating dinner together as a family is a powerful strategy for helping your child achieve success. Listen to what your child tells you during dinner. You will be able to perceive if your child is doing and feeling well, or you will notice if some problems are occurring. Use this time to stay connected with your child. Make the dinner table a safe and enjoyable place where everyone can relax, enjoy the food, and share their stories. The time you spend with your child during dinner will strengthen his or her self-worth, improve your relationship, and help your child be successful.

12

Give Praise and Show Affection Daily

Justin is hungry for attention. He is an honor roll student with perfect attendance. He volunteers to help his teacher with tasks in the classroom, and he is willing to stay after school to help the teacher as well. He thrives on the attention his teacher gives him. He replays in his head the teacher's comments of praise and appreciation that are given to him each day. Justin feels his teacher is the only one who really notices him and cares about him.

Many of our students are desperate for attention, affection and praise. Parents often focus so much on the external matters of parenting involving discipline and guidance that they forget to focus time on their child's emotional needs. Consequently, children turn to others to get these needs met. Schools often have to discipline children for inappropriate expressions of affection. These children are craving affection, and they are willing to risk punishment to get their needs met. Schools are also filled with students who are desperate for attention, and they will either misbehave to be noticed or latch on to an adult who gives them the attention they need. The home is where students must get their needs met for attention and affection. This will help prevent confusion, embarrassment, and problems for students in the school.

AFFECTION

Amanda loves going to Tanisha's house. Tanisha's family is always hugging and holding hands. She can tell they really care about each other. Amanda's house is so different. She cannot remember the last time her parents hugged her or each other.

Children need to experience affection from their parents. Hugs, kisses and touching are essential elements to children's emotional development. Many parents avoid demonstrating too much affection for their children because they fear it might make their children weak, or they themselves are uncomfortable with expressing affection. Yet, if children do not get their needs met at home with touch and affection, they will turn elsewhere to other adults or peers to get this need met—often in unhealthy ways. Parents can meet their children's emotional need for affection while teaching them the appropriate boundaries for expressing affection. Children can be taught to listen to their instinct (the feeling in their stomachs) and judge whether or not affection is appropriate. Healthy affection with children does not equate with sexual abuse. There is a significant difference between kissing a child goodnight, hugging him or her, or holding a child's hand and crossing the line to inappropriate affection. Expressing affection with children is about meeting their needs for touch and affection; it is not about meeting the needs of an adult. If you have a difficult time expressing affection with your child in healthy ways, talk to a trusted professional or health care provider about your concerns. Your child's emotional health is dependent on your own level of healthiness.

PRAISE

Dad: Fantastic job, Joshua. You really did a great job in the play.

Joshua: No I didn't. I forgot some of my lines.

Dad: I couldn't tell. That is the sign of a gifted actor: one who forgets lines but who covers up the mistake so the audience cannot tell. You really did well.

Joshua: Thanks Dad. I guess it was pretty good. I can't wait until the next play.

Children need to hear praise from their parents. Genuine compliments to your child on who he or she is as a person or on something your child has accomplished will enhance your child's esteem. Children who grow up in homes where they receive positive feedback from their parents will develop the confidence needed to excel in school. These children will believe that they can do well in school, and this positive thinking will propel them towards success. Children who come from homes where their accomplishments are not acknowledged, or where they are often compared negatively with others, will struggle to do well in school. These children come to school with a deficit in their self-esteem, and this deficit is difficult to overcome. They do not believe that they have the resources and internal skills needed to be successful. Parents have the power to enhance a healthy self-esteem in their children, or they have the power to break their children's self-esteem. Use your power wisely. Make a conscious effort to praise your child each day. Help your child discover something that he or she can do well, and praise him or her for the success. Encourage your child to try new things and pursue these areas of interest. Your child's successes will build his or her confidence and lead to a stronger self-esteem. Praise can be directed towards a task your child has completed, or it can be simply about who your child is as a person. The following examples give simple praises that parents can use with their children.

- You play so well with your sister. You are a good role model for her.
- You did a nice job making your bed. It makes your room look very neat.
- I appreciate you taking the time to visit with your grandmother. She got the chance to see what a wonderful person you are.
- This paper you wrote for English is very good. I really have an excellent writer for a daughter.
- I am so lucky to have you as a son. You are a blessing to me.

Simple daily, genuine compliments will create miracles in your child's life. Your child's self-confidence will grow stronger, and he or she will be more successful in school.

Make it a practice each day to praise your child and be affectionate. These simple acts will be major influences in helping your child achieve success.

13

Establish Clear Expectations for Behavior

Adam: Mom, can I go outside to play?

Mom: No, you did not clean your room yesterday. I told you if you did not clean your room yesterday, you could not go outside today.

Adam: That is not fair. Everyone else is outside playing.

Mom: But, you did not clean your room.

Adam: What am I supposed to do all day in the house?

Mom: You can clean your room first, and then you can help me clean the kitchen.

Adam: I don't want to spend all day cleaning! I want to play outside!

Mom: Adam, I am sorry that you made the choice yesterday to not clean your room. But, you knew the consequence, so you can't go outside.

Adam: I hate you!

Mom (to herself): It won't be the last time.

Disciplining children can be one of the least favorite aspects of parenting. Many parents see discipline as a chore and as an interaction that puts parents at odds with children. Discipline, though, is one of the best teaching tools parents can use with their children. Parents are the primary facilitators for discipline. Children who are disciplined well by their parents will have an easier time achieving success in school and in society.

Discipline begins when children are toddlers, and it continues until adulthood. We start disciplining children when they are young, because the consequences become more severe as children get older. It is better and safer for children to learn how to make good choices when they are younger. Discipline teaches self-control, and it teaches children the natural consequences of behavior. Discipline provides structure and consistency for children while they learn how to live cooperatively in society. Children need the structure of discipline to feel safe and secure. Disciplining your child should be looked on as teaching opportunities. The lessons learned at home will transfer to the school setting, and these lessons will help your child have more success in school.

BE PREPARED

Karla: I hope our children are better behaved than my sister's children.

Ben: They will be. Your sister doesn't spank her kids, but we won't make that mistake.

Karla: No, I don't want to spank our children. I think we can discipline them without spanking.

Ben: My dad spanked me plenty of times. It was the only way I would behave. If you don't spank children, they will never learn. But, we don't have to worry about that until we have kids.

Effectively disciplining your child takes preparation. You should decide before your child is born what kind of discipline style you will use with your child. Many schools, churches and community agencies teach effective discipline techniques to parents. There are also numerous books available on effective discipline strategies. Two popular book series are *How to Behave So Your Children Will, Too* by Sal Severe (www.howtobehave.com) and Love and Logic Parenting books by Jim Fay and Foster Cline (www.loveandlogic.com). Learn about recommended discipline techniques, and discuss your strategies and values with your partner so that you both will agree to follow the same discipline style. You will be more effective with your discipline style if you and your partner decide early in your child's life what kinds of discipline techniques you want to utilize. It is never too late, though, to begin using effective and consistent discipline techniques with your child. If your child is older, it might take longer before you see positive results. Yet, if you are consistent with your strategies, you will see results.

BE CONSISTENT WITH CONSEQUENCES

The key element in disciplining your child is being consistent with consequences. Your child will make the wrong choices—some children more often than others. Regardless of what choices he or she makes, there have to be consequences for the actions. Sometimes, the consequences are positive, i.e.: studying for a test and earning an A, or the consequences can be negative, i.e.: not studying for a test and failing the exam. The key to learning for children is to understand which consequence will result from which choice.

Parents often have trouble with discipline because they are not consistent and firm with consequences. It is essential to follow through with consequences--regardless of how difficult it is to remain firm--so that children will learn the lessons they need to learn.

Vincent: Dad, I need $300 to pay for summer school.

Dad: Where are you going to get it?

Vincent: Daaad. I'm asking you for the money.

Dad: I didn't fail my classes. I don't need to go to summer school. Why should I pay for the classes?

Vincent: Because you are my father.

Dad: And, as your father, I told you all year long to complete your homework and study for tests. You thought you could get by without any effort, and you failed two classes. If you want to be promoted, you have to go to summer school. If you want to go to summer school, you have to pay for it. So, how are you going to pay for it?

Vincent: I guess I have to get a job.

Dad: Good decision. There are plenty of our neighbors who would love for you to mow their lawns this summer. You can do that or figure out something else. I know you will be able to work this out.

Vincent's father wanted to rescue his son from consequences, but he knew that if he did Vincent would not learn anything from this experience. Vincent not only paid the full summer school bill, he also passed his classes so that he could go to the next grade. He never had to attend summer school again. Rescuing children from consequences does not benefit them. This is the only way children learn how to make good choices. Parents who hover around their children and rescue them from the bad things in life are not protecting them. They are, instead, preventing them from learning how to accept responsibility and be successful in school and society.

Be clear with your child about the consequences of his or her behavior. You also want to be sure that you can live with the consequences as well. If you tell your child that the family will not go to a movie if the trash is not taken outside, be prepared to stay home if your child does not take the trash outside. The type of consequence is not as important as consistently allowing your child to experience consequences. Yet, the consequence has to be one that will make your child not want to make the negative choice in the future. When your child learns that he or she will always experience a consequence for a choice, then your child will quickly learn to make the choices that result in positive consequences. This learning will transfer to the school setting, and your child will be able to better resist peer pressure and make healthy choices.

AVOID PARENTING EXTREMES

Joseph is not going to allow his children to grow up without learning respect and responsibility. He believes in being a strict disciplinarian, and he does not allow his children to make decisions for themselves because they might make the wrong decisions. If his children misbehave, he gives them strict consequences so that they will never make the mistake again. His children fear him, and Joseph believes that is the best way to make children behave.

An effective discipline style will allow your child to learn how to make positive choices, accept responsibility, and maintain dignity. Parents can help children achieve these milestones, or they can prevent them from occurring. Ineffective discipline occurs when parents are either too strict or too permissive.

When a parent is too strict, children are not allowed to make choices and learn from their mistakes. Children are not given the opportunities to develop a sense of responsibility and develop decision-making skills because all of the decisions are made for them. These children are not given a role in their own development, and consequently, as adolescents, they are deficient in their ability to self-regulate their actions. They are more susceptible to peer pressure because they are used to someone else making their decisions for them. They do not know how to set limits and trust their judgment. These students are more likely to make poor decisions that will cause trouble for them in school and society. They often eventually rebel against the rigidity of their childhood and participate in dangerous behaviors as teenagers or young adults.

Conversely, when parents are too permissive in their discipline styles, they do not provide the boundaries and structure children need. They allow children the freedom to make all of the decisions without any guidance. These children become overwhelmed with this freedom and they often are unable to regulate their behavior. I have had many students who are sexually active and/or abuse alcohol and drugs because their parents do not accept the responsibility of setting boundaries and expectations. They allow their children to grow-up unsupervised. Children need to have a role in developing their decision-making skills, but they do not need to be left alone to learn the skills. Parents must guide children through adolescence by teaching them how to make good choices based on a limited number of options. As children get older and they show that they can handle the responsibility of making decisions, they can be given more options from which to choose when making a decision.

REMAIN EMPATHETIC

Efrem is having a hard time. Kids are making fun of him at school because his voice is changing. He finally had enough, and he hit a kid. Efrem's father was angry when he received a call from the vice principal about Efrem's behavior, and he was told that Efrem was suspended from school. He reminded himself, though, to talk to Efrem and find out what happened. When he picked Efrem up from school, Efrem would not talk at first. After Efrem's father reassured him that he wanted to help him work through this problem, Efrem finally told his father how embarrassed he is in class. Efrem admitted that he hit the other student because he couldn't take being teased anymore. Efrem's father was able to listen to him and tell him how sorry he is that Efrem is embarrassed. He went on to say that he is sorry that Efrem is suspended because that means he has to miss school and spend the day at his grandmother's house doing chores. Efrem's father then turned the situation into a teaching opportunity and his father went on to discuss with Efrem about what other choices he could make the next time he is feeling embarrassed.

Being a child is tough. In addition to having to learn how to function effectively in society by learning about the rules and acceptable behavior, children are quickly undergoing physical changes that are transforming their bodies from children to adults. The hormonal changes that occur during this time can be overwhelming for children. Children need a lot of empathy from adults in their lives while they are growing and learning. They will make mistakes. This is how they learn. Adults can help make this process less harsh by being empathetic with children when they make mistakes and experience consequences. Telling a child, "I am sorry that you won't be able to go on the field trip because you were sent to the office," is far more empathetic than saying, "You deserve to miss the field trip." Children need to know that adults are on their side regardless of the situation. They need to feel that parents still care about them and understand their feelings. The consequences children experience will be the lessons that they need to learn to make a better choices in the future. Parents who degrade or embarrass children for poor choices will only chip away at children's self-esteem. Parents can be disappointed in their children's choices, but this can be expressed in an empathetic manner. Yelling at children will only cause them to recoil and stop listening. If children are yelled at frequently, they will eventually stop listening all together. Children respond to empathy, love and support. When they receive this from their parents, children will be more likely to listen and make better choices.

Disciplining your child is not about punishing him or her; it is about teaching your child how to make choices that lead to success. When you discipline your child, those moments are golden opportunities for your child to learn how to make better choices. As a parent, your role is to help your child learn how to make good choices while providing him or her the structure needed to develop into a healthy adult. When your child develops the confidence and skills needed to make good choices, this will carry over into the school setting and in peer relations where your child will achieve greater success.

14

Ask for Help

Counselor: Mr. Winters, we have noticed a change in Michael's behavior that concerns us. Is there anything we should know that could be affecting his progress in school?

Mr. Winters: No, there is nothing going on.

Counselor: Michael is falling asleep in class; he is disrespectful to adults; his grades are failing; and today he was in a fight. This is not the behavior that we expect from Michael. Last year he did so well, but this year we have seen a change, and he is really struggling.

Mr. Winters: Michael is fine. I will punish him at home for fighting. There is nothing you need to know.

Counselor: Well, we really care about Michael, and we want to help him to do well at school. We have a lot of resources available for children who are having difficulties. But, we need to work with you to help Michael do well.

Mr. Winters: I already told you that Michael is fine. I need to get to work.

One of the hardest things for many parents to do is ask for help. Some parents are embarrassed that they are not able to handle all of their children's problems by themselves. Other parents are fiercely protective of their privacy, and they do not want outsiders to know about their family problems—even at the expense of their children's well-being. Many parents, though, understand that there are numerous obstacles today that interfere with a child's success, and it takes several resources at times to help a child through a difficult period. The need for privacy or the embarrassment of having to ask for help is understandable. There was a time when people were expected to work out their own problems and asking for help was a sign of weakness. That attitude, though, has changed, and there are many useful resources available to help parents through difficult times.

There are countless reasons why today's children might struggle for success. Children are feeling pressured to excel and be the best. They are constantly comparing themselves to others, and many do not feel that they are smart enough, pretty enough, athletic enough, or funny enough to be worthy. The media has pressured children to compete with an unrealistic ideal of what it means to be accepted. When children begin internalizing the belief that they are not as good as everyone else, they can become depressed, and they are more likely to turn to unhealthy behaviors as a way of coping with their feelings.

Children are also affected by the actions of others around them. Children can struggle when they are experiencing stress in the home either from divorce, death, the substance abuse of a family member, the ill-health of a family member or any other host of problems that can occur. The home is supposed to be a child's safety net from the challenges of school and society. Yet, if being at home becomes a challenge, children have no safe place to rest their heads. Children often do not let others know how much stress they are experiencing due to home problems because they want to keep family matters private. These children struggle to cope with their family problems without help from anyone else, and this can be overwhelming.

The same is true if children are experiencing difficulties at school or with peers. Children who struggle with learning or who are not successful in connecting socially with their peers need help in overcoming these obstacles. Yet, children often do not ask for help in these areas because they are embarrassed that they are not able to be independently successful. These types of problems can be overwhelming for children. If they do not learn the skills needed to cope with these problems, they might be drawn to unhealthy ways of coping with their consuming emotions.

Parents, ideally, are the first to notice when their children are struggling with emotions. If you notice an unexplained change in your child's behavior, talk to you child and discuss different kinds of feelings with your child. Be willing to consult with a school counselor, health care worker, minister, teacher or other professional who is familiar with your child if you have concerns. The following signs can help you determine if your child might need additional help.

YOUNG CHILDREN

- Decline in grades
- Excessive anxiety or worrying
- Nightmares
- Temper tantrums and/or change in behavior
- Unexplained physical complaints
- Comments about disappearing or suicide

OLDER CHILDREN

- Decline in grades
- Changes in sleep and/or eating habits
- Unexplained physical complaints
- Change in mood and behavior
- Sexual activity
- Alcohol and/or drug abuse
- Self-harm or threats to others
- Unusual thoughts, feelings or obsessions

If these problems persist, consultation with a professional might be useful in determining if your child needs counseling services.

Parents often do not notice that their children are in crisis until it is too late. They then try to use their best parenting techniques to help their children, but the strategies are not effective. Additionally, a technique that might have worked with one sibling is ineffective for another, or a strategy that might have worked the previous year has no impact now. If your child is struggling and you no longer know what to do to help, ask for help. Your child's school counselor is an excellent resource to work with you in helping your child through difficult times. Some parents are hesitant to consult with counselors because they fear the counselor will learn about the family's secrets, or the counselor will try to turn their child against them. The priority of a counselor is the well-being of children, so his or her focus is on helping children become successful and healthy. Children need a strong and healthy relationship with their parents for support and success, and supporting this relationship is one of the goals of good counselors. Counselors do not try to divide families because that would be detrimental to the children. Be open to counseling for both your child and family if it is recommended. The issues of today sometime require that parents work with professionals to help their children through crises. If your child has a time where he or she is showing signs of distress, consult with your school counselor or another professional for guidance so that you can help your child progress through difficult times and find success.

For further information:
American Academy of Pediatrics, www.aap.org
American Counseling Association, www.counseling.org
American Psychiatric Association, www.psych.org/public_info
American Psychological Association, www.apa.org

15

Teach Personal Safety

Joanna will not get out of bed to go to school. She has been doing this all week, and her mother is getting frustrated. Joanna used to be the first one awake every morning, and she was never late for school. Now, she is always feeling sick, and her mother has to drag her out of the house each morning to go to school. Joanna's mother never expected to have this kind of trouble with a second grader. She has asked Joanna several times, "What is the matter?" but Joanna just shrugs her shoulders and says, "Nothing." She hopes Joanna will soon get over her moodiness. She is tired of their new morning ritual.

Childhood is a confusing time for both parents and children. It is difficult to tell at times if children are behaving differently because they are children or because something is bothering them. Parents have the delicate task of knowing when to allow children the space to be alone with their thoughts and when to push for answers when there is a concern. If open communication has already been established between parents and children, and if children have been given the tools needed to know how to maintain their personal safety, parents can feel more confident in their ability to judge when their children need help.

Childhood is supposed to be a time of innocence and trust. Unfortunately, children are easy targets for abuse because they are so

85

trusting and vulnerable. Children who do become victims of abuse or harassment might find it difficult to concentrate in school and behave appropriately. Parents must teach their children about personal safety so that they are able to protect themselves from people who are abusive. Children often lack the skills needed to protect themselves from harm, and if they are not educated on how to stay safe, they will not know how to handle potentially dangerous situations. Additionally, children lack the vocabulary needed to tell an adult if they are being abused and they need help. Teaching children how to respond to abuse will help keep them safe.

Children who become victims of abuse may not tell an adult what is happening, but their behavior will change. Parents might notice a difference in mood and attitude, but it is often dismissed as childhood moodiness. Children give clues when they are troubled, and parents need to stay connected to their children in order to notice the clues. The abuse children experience can involve child abuse, bullying, hazing, sexual harassment, and relationship violence. This abuse can occur at home, in school, in the neighborhood, or at friends' houses. Parents cannot protect their children every moment of every day, so children need to learn the skills required to protect themselves. Children as young as preschool age can be taught what feels right and wrong, and they can learn what to do if something feels wrong.

Children who are victims of some type of abuse typically show signs that they are in crisis. These signs can include:
- physical complaints of headaches, stomach aches or body pains;
- resistance to attending school;
- failing grades;
- withdrawal from the family;
- sadness, mood changes, and frequent crying;
- secretiveness;
- more tired than usual and a change in sleep habits;
- change in appetite and/or weight;
- loss of interest in activities;
- change in friends;

- drug and/or alcohol use;
- fighting; and/or
- exhibiting sexually inappropriate behavior or knowledge.

Children who are victims of abuse can be affected socially and emotionally. Victims of abuse do not believe that they can do anything to change the situation; they feel powerless. They are often embarrassed or confused about the situation, and they do not ask for help. Feelings of hopelessness will eventually consume these children, and they become at-risk for being depressed or suicidal and/or they become aggressive towards others. These children have a difficult time focusing in school, and many of them resist going to school. When children are taught personal safety skills, they can protect themselves from being victims. They know what to do if they are ever in a situation of danger. Situations where children might become victims include child abuse, bullying, hazing, sexual harassment and relationship violence.

CHILD ABUSE

Jake's father has noticed that Jake has been gaining weight recently. He seems to have less energy, and all Jake wants to wear is baggy clothes. Jake's father is concerned about his son's weight gain, but he does not want to embarrass him by talking about it. Jake's father decides to just have healthier food around the house and to try and get Jake to be more active.

Children are killed every day in America as a result of abuse. Too many children are suffering from some form of child abuse, and much of it is unreported. Most child abuse occurs in the home where parents or caregivers physically or emotionally abuse their children, or the children's physical needs are neglected. These are very damaging environments for children to live in, as the effects will last a lifetime. Many children have permanent physical damage from abuse, and too many children are killed from being the victims of child abuse. If you are aware of incidences of child abuse involving a child you know, you must contact your local child welfare agency or the police for assistance. Children do not have the ability to protect themselves from their parents, and they are dependent upon other adults for protection if necessary. If you are abusing your child in any manner, you must get help immediately. Consult with your health care provider or another professional for help. Your child's health and safety depend on your ability to provide a safe and nurturing home.

Sexual abuse is a crime that affects too many children. A child who is sexually abused will struggle throughout his or her life to have healthy and trusting relationships as an adult. Sexual abuse can occur from a parent, but it is also the one type of abuse that can occur without a parent being aware. Sexual abuse includes exposing a child to pornography, having a child undress, pose or perform in a sexual manner, using inappropriate sexual language, touching inappropriately and/or sexual assault. Children usually trust their abusers, and they are forced to keep the abuse a secret either through threats or other forms of manipulation. Parents often trust the abuser as well, and they have no idea that this trusted adult is abusing their child. Children need to be taught appropriate boundaries. They can be taught to listen to their instinct (the feeling in their stomach) to decide if something feels right or wrong. Children of all ages can be taught the following rules to protect themselves.

- You have the right to say "No" to anyone who is trying to hurt you or do something to make you feel uncomfortable. You do not have to be polite to an adult if he or she is trying to hurt you or make you feel uncomfortable.
- You have the right to get away from a situation that is not comfortable and ask for help. You do not need to stay with an adult who is trying to hurt you or do things that do not feel right. Listen to your instinct and trust what it is telling you. If something does not feel right, get away from it.
- When someone tries to do something to you that does not feel right, ask another adult for help and keep asking until someone can help you. You might have to ask several people for help but do not give up until someone hears you and helps you.
- Do not keep secrets about someone hurting you, even if the person tries to scare you into keeping the secret. Secrets are dif-

ferent from surprises. You can keep a surprise from your parents, but do not keep secrets from your parents. They need to know what is going on so they can help you.

Children need to learn that their bodies belong to them, and no one (people they know or strangers) has a right to touch their private parts. Assure your child that you will believe him or her if he or she tells you about being abused. Children are easily confused because they usually trust the adult who is abusing them, and some children know their parents trust the adult as well. It is confusing to have a trusted adult do something that does not feel right. Perpetrators of sexual abuse need children to trust them in order for the abuse to happen. Tell your child that it is your job to protect him or her, so you need to know if he or she is being hurt. Do not force young children to hug or kiss anyone. Children often do not feel comfortable hugging or kissing relatives, and their feelings should be respected. If a child is forced to show affection to someone, then that child has learned that his or her feelings do not matter and should be ignored. This is a dangerous lesson to teach a child as he or she might ignore important feelings later if someone is doing something to the child that is harmful. Well-meaning adults or friends who want to hug a child might be offended if the child refuses the affection, but honoring a child's feelings is far more important than humoring an adult.

Also, talk to your teenager about date rape. Explain to your teenager that he or she needs to trust his or her instincts when on dates or at parties, and leave any situation that does not feel right. Teach your teenager that he or she has the right to say "No" to a date if something does not feel comfortable.

Children of all ages must learn that they must always tell their parents or another adult when anyone tries to touch them in a way that does not feel right. Children need to know how to protect themselves from becoming a victim, and they need to believe that they can go to an adult if there is a problem. This is the only way children can be protected from being victims of sexual abuse. For more information about child abuse prevention, consult with your school counselor or contact www.childabuse.com; www.childabuse.org; or www.

preventchildabuse.org.

BULLYING

Teddy hates going to school. He used to love waking up each morning to go to school, but this year he dreads it. There are some boys that make fun of Teddy for how he dresses, and they harass him at school. They have even threatened to beat him up. Teddy has told his father what is happening, but his father told him to just ignore it. His father said if he ignored the boys, they would quit bothering him. Teddy tried this, but it has not worked. He doesn't know what else to do, and he just can't take it anymore.

Millions of children are bullied in school each year. Bullying behaviors can include one child looking at another child in a certain way to cause the other child to be in fear; bullying can be in the form of verbal harassment such as name calling, spreading rumors and teasing; bullying can include purposely excluding a child from activities; or bullying can involve physical attacks from one child to another. Bullying is an ongoing series of physical and/or verbal abuses in which one child has power over the other child. Boy bullies tend to be involved in physical intimidation or threats directed at boys and girls. Girl bullies usually target other girls with verbal bullying. The victims of bullying are upset by the harassment while the aggressors are either unaffected or pleased by the incidents. Bullying is not normal adolescent behavior, and it can be harmful to the victim. Bullies often target children who are different than other children. This can include differences in appearance such as weight, height, wearing eyeglasses, hearing aides, ethnic background, mannerisms or clothing. It can also include differences in a child's social ability where a child is very shy, easily intimidated, or has learning difficulties. Sometimes, there is no known reason why a bully targets a victim. You can teach your child, though, to protect him or herself from being bullied.

- Help your child develop confidence and strength. Praise your child often, and teach him or her that he or she has the skills to handle difficult situations. Teach your child how to silently reassure him or herself that when confronted by a bully, the situation can be successfully resolved.

- Teach your child to make eye contact with the bully, be assertive, and say, "Stop right now. I will tell an adult what you are doing." Have your child practice saying this with a strong voice so he or she will be prepared if confronted by a bully. Do not encourage your child to fight back as this might make the situation worse.
- Tell your child to ask for help from an adult when a bullying situation occurs. Impress upon your child that it is okay to ask for help when someone is being a bully, and it is not the victim's fault.
- Teach your child to trust his or her instincts. If something or someone does not "feel" right, get away immediately. Girls, especially, need to be taught that they do not have to be polite when they are in an uncomfortable or frightening situation.
- Teach your child to avoid unknown or unsafe areas in school and in the neighborhood. Your child needs to learn to not put him or herself in a location where bullying might occur. Encourage your child to be with friends when walking to and from school. Bullies are less likely to target children in a group.
- Talk openly with your child about what bullying means, and encourage your child to tell you when he or she sees bullying happening at school. If you are aware of another child being bullied, contact school officials (U.S. Department of Health and Human Services).

Cyberbullying is the newest method of bullying. Children are using the Internet to harass, intimidate, humiliate and target others for bullying. Children can spread rumors, gossip, slander, threats and post misleading pictures through the internet. This type of bullying can be more vicious because it occurs in the homes of children, and it can be witnessed by many people through the Internet. Victims of cyberbullying are reluctant to tell their parents about the harassment because they do not want their parents interfering with their computer activities. Cyberbullying can lead to serious consequences, though, as victims feel powerless to stop the online bullying. Children who are victims can become withdrawn, depressed and suicidal as a result of the bullying. Parents must be aware of their children's internet activities to protect them from the dangers that are always present online. If your child is a victim of cyberbullying, the following tips can guide you on how to deal with the harassment.

- Teach your child how to use chat rooms and blogs safely to minimize the risk of becoming bullied.
- Educate your child about cyberbullying, and instruct your child to share with you any cyberbullying messages that are seen on the Internet. Print and save these messages.
- Meet with school officials if you believe your child is being cyberbullied by another student who attends your child's school.
- Teach your child that reading and forwarding messages whose intent is to cyberbully another person is not acceptable. Children should not passively watch another child be victimized on the Internet. Instruct your child to talk to you about any cyberbullying observed online.
- More information about Internet safety can be found in Lesson 17: Monitor Technology

Additionally, teach your child to treat others with respect and consideration and avoid participating in or observing the bullying of others on the Internet. More information about cyberbullying can be found at www.cyberbully.org and www.wiredsafety.org.

A common but unrecognized type of bullying is relational bullying. This type of bullying occurs in a friendship, and it involves one child exerting power over another by making demands on the child in order to maintain the relationship. The demands can include:

- one child telling the other child to ignore or be mean to a third child;
- one child requiring another child to do things for the child/bully, ie: homework; and/or
- one child forcing the other child to dress, talk or behave in a certain manner to maintain the friendship.

This type of bullying has been observed in children as young as three years of age. Teach your child at an early age that respect is an essential part of any friendship, and a bullying situation occurs if a child is placing conditions on a friendship in order for the relationship to be maintained.

If your child is a victim of bullying, whether it is in person or on the Internet, he or she might be too embarrassed to tell you. Encourage your child to talk about his or her experiences by asking what it is like to walk to school or the bus stop; how do kids behave on the playground; and what goes on before and after school. Talk to your child about what makes a bully, and ask if there are any kids in the neighborhood or school who fit the description. Ask you child what he or she knows about cyberbullying and share facts about how destructive bullying can be for a child. If you find out students are bullying, contact your child's school to ask for assistance. Talk to your child's school about their policy on bullying. Find out what programs the school has in place to prevent or deal with bullying. Some schools are very proactive in preventing bullying while other schools have not dealt with the problem yet. As a parent, you can encourage your school to address the problem of bullying, and educate students and staff about this issue. The most effective way to stop bullying is to educate students and staff through anti-bullying programs or tolerance programs that are implemented school-wide. These programs can teach school personnel, students and parents how to create a climate of compassion and acceptance so that bullying is no longer tolerated. When students learn about the importance of treating others with kindness, they will begin to exhibit positive traits in their schools and bullying behaviors will decline. Bullies draw their power from other students who observe or join in the bullying of another. When other students decide to no longer support bullies, the school environment will change to one of compassion, and bullies will be less likely to continue harassing students. This is the most powerful method for eliminating bullying in schools.

You might be the parent of a bully. Bullies learn from their experiences. If a sibling or another relative bullies your child at home, he or she might use the same behaviors at school. Characteristics of

potential bullies include:
- attempting to dominate others;
- being a poor winner or loser;
- enjoying when others are in fear or pain;
- being manipulative and hiding behaviors from adults;
- blaming others for problems;
- being aggressive and violent;
- lacking empathy; and
- having uncontrollable anger (U.S. Department of Health and Human Services).

If you suspect your child might be a bully, talk to your school counselor or another professional. If your child does not get help, he or she might develop academic, social and emotional problems. An intervention with a professional will help your child understand his or her feelings, and your child can learn healthy ways to get his or her needs met.

For more information on bullying in schools, contact your school administration or the National Parent Teacher Association website at www.pta.org/bullying.

HAZING

Larry does not know what to do. He has wanted to play football ever since he could walk. He planned on playing high school football and then getting a scholarship to play in college. He even imagines himself playing in the pros. If he doesn't play football, he doesn't know what he will do. But, this isn't what he expected. He is a freshman playing on the junior varsity, and the other players are harassing him. They hit him, call him names, and steal his clothes while he showers. He thought it would eventually stop, but the players just keep harassing him. He doesn't want to tell the coach or his parents about the harassment because that would make it worse. He is thinking of quitting football.

Hazing is a growing trend stretching from college to middle schools. Hazing has typically been limited to behaviors seen on college campuses, but more and more incidences of hazing are occurring in the lower grades. Hazing occurs when a group of students coerce or force someone to do something that will intentionally embarrass, humiliate or cause physical discomfort for the person either for the group's enjoyment and/or to make the person prove he or she is "worthy" to be a member of the group. Hazing can include:

- demeaning a student in public;
- requiring a student to address group members in a specific manner;
- requiring a student to wear embarrassing clothing;
- requiring a student to be a servant to another student;
- forcing a student to disrobe;
- requiring a student to consume alcohol or drugs;
- physically harming a student; and/or
- ridiculing a student.

Hazing can include numerous other actions. The purpose is generally to demean a person for the enjoyment of the group.

Hazing is found in a wide variety of groups including athletes, cheerleaders, fine arts groups, church groups, gangs, social clubs, vocational groups, journalism clubs and political groups. Hazing often leads to negative consequences including fighting, injuries, academic difficulties, behavior problems, eating and sleeping problems, isolation and death. Hazing can destroy self-confidence, self-esteem, trust, friendships, and organizations. Hazing has powerful consequences, and parents together with schools must work to eliminate hazing from campuses.

Hazing can be prevented if attention is focused on the problem. Parents, students, school officials and the community need to be educated about what defines hazing and what to do if it occurs. Students engaged in hazing should be strongly disciplined by the school and/or law enforcement. Educate your child about hazing. Let him or her know what it is and what to do if he or she encounters hazing. Your child should learn not to participate in the hazing of another student or allow him or herself to be subject to hazing. If it does occur, your child should tell you immediately so you can help resolve the incident.

Mothers Against School Hazing (MASH) will give you more information on hazing at www.mashinc.org.

SEXUAL HARASSMENT

Sandra is embarrassed. She is in the fourth grade, and she already has to wear a bra. None of the other girls in her class are wearing bras yet, and she is very self-conscious about her changing body. She hoped no one would notice that she wears a bra, but some boys have started popping her bra strap during P.E. Everyone laughs when they do it. She laughs with them so they do not know how much it upsets her. But, each time it happens, Sandra is humiliated.

Sexual harassment happens in all grades. Sexual harassment is not about sex; it is about using sex to exercise power, control and intimidation over another person. Students learn how to do this at an early age thanks to exposure from the media and observing others who exhibit inappropriate behaviors. Sexual harassment can range from a suggestive statement or noise or inappropriate grabbing to aggressive sexual assault. Both boys and girls can be the victims and the perpetrators of sexual harassment, and it can happen at any age.

Children need to learn at an early age to trust their instinct. If someone makes comments or touches them in a way that is not comfortable, they have a right to tell the person to stop. Children also need to know which adults they can talk to if someone is sexually harassing them. Sexual harassment of a student can get out of control if an adult does not intervene. Comments about a girl who is "easy" or a boy who is a "virgin" can spread as rumors around a school, and it is humiliating for the child. The Internet has taken sexual harassment to a new level. Students can start a sexually harassing rumor about a student on the Internet, and it will spread quickly. Once a rumor gets started on the Internet, it is difficult to stop. Children need to stop any harassment immediately by reporting it to their parents and school officials. Your child needs to believe that you are willing to listen and believe him or her if harassment is occurring. Talk to school officials with your child about the harassment because this is a sensitive issue that can cause embarrassment for your child. Be the one person your child can depend on for support and comfort.

Parents need to educate their children about what is sexual harassment, and teach them that it is unacceptable to make harassing comments, gestures or actions towards another student. Students who are taught empathy are less likely to target another student in an attempt to embarrass the student. Harassment can be prevented when parents, students and schools work together to prevent the behavior from occurring. For more information on sexual harassment in schools, consult with your school counselor or contact the American Association of University Women website at www.aauw.org.

RELATIONSHIP VIOLENCE

Mandisa loves her boyfriend. She cannot believe how lucky she is that Ray chose to be with her. Things were great at first, but it has been more difficult lately. Ray won't let her talk to her friends, and he gets very angry when she even looks at another guy. He has hit her a couple of times when he got angry, but he is always sorry afterwards. Mandisa and Ray have three classes together, and he is always watching her. She is afraid to look at the wrong person or say the wrong thing. She can't tell her parents that Ray has hit her because they will make her break-up with him. She loves Ray, and she knows that he does not mean to hurt her; he just has trouble controlling his anger. He promised the last time, though, to never hit her again.

Children are often anxious to have a boyfriend or girlfriend— even in elementary school. Children have learned from society that they are acceptable and worthy if they have a boyfriend or girlfriend. Consequently, some children find themselves in abusive relationships because they are afraid to be alone. For these children, it is better to be abused in a relationship than it is to be safe but alone.

Children learn what constitutes a healthy relationship by watching the quality of relationships of their parents. Children learn how to be in a relationship by watching how their parents talk to each other, respect each other and handle conflicts. Children who have parents who model violence, aggression and disrespect in relationships are more likely to become involved in violent relationships. Children who learn from their parents that conflicts can be handled peacefully and respecting your partner is essential in healthy relationships will take these lessons into their own relationships.

You are the primary teacher for you child about healthy relationships. Your words and actions will show your child what it means to be in a healthy relationship.

Healthy relationships involve:
• respecting your partner's ideas, beliefs, goals and family;
• trusting that your partner will treat you well and be dependable;
• being honest about feelings, thoughts and actions;
• treating your partner fairly and compromising often;
• resolving conflicts non-violently through discussions of perspectives and feelings;
• allowing your partner to pursue his or her own interest and friendships while you pursue yours; and
• maintaining good communication with your partner.

Unhealthy relationships involve:
• lack of trust leading to jealousy and accusations;
• a controlling partner who limits activities, friends and choices;
• resolving conflicts through yelling and hitting;
• refusing to talk about problems;
• physical, sexual and emotional abuse;
• cheating on partner;
• humiliating and/or embarrassing partner in front of others; and
• one partner using fear to control the other.

Teach your child what it means to be in a healthy relationship by ensuring that your own relationships are healthy. Also, talk to your child about his or her relationships. If your child is secretive about his or her relationships, or if you notice a negative change in your child's personality since becoming involved with another person, talk to your child about the relationship and consult with a professional for guidance if necessary. Your child might be experiencing normal adolescent phases or he or she might be in a relationship that is unhealthy.

Children who feel good about themselves are less likely to become involved with someone who is disrespectful towards them. Help your child develop a healthy self-esteem by praising him or her, finding activities for your child to participate in which he or she is successful, and spending quality time with your child. Your child will be with people who are respectful and considerate if your child believes that he or she deserves to be treated well. You can teach your child to have high standards for friends and partners.

Healthy relationships require maturity and skill. Most children become involved in romantic relationships when they are still too young to have the skills needed to build a good relationship. Use common sense when deciding if your child is old enough to become involved with a boyfriend or girlfriend, and maintain open communication with your child about his or her experiences. Your child will appreciate knowing that regardless of the choices he or she makes, you are there to help him or her learn and grow from the experiences. For more information about teen relationship violence, consult with your school counselor or contact www.kidshealth.org or the Women's Law. org website at www.womenslaw.org/teens.htm.

Parents usually do everything they can to protect their children from harm. Yet, children do need to learn how to maneuver in society and protect themselves if necessary. Teaching children the personal safety skills needed to handle difficult situations and helping them be prepared for these circumstances will provide children with the tools they need to be safe. Parents cannot always be physically present with their children, but good parenting involves teaching children how to protect themselves when their parents are not around.

16

Know Your Child's Friends

Dad: Luis, why don't you invite some of your friends to go with us to the park tomorrow?

Luis: Nah, that's okay.

Dad: Come on, Luis. We can play football and eat lunch at the park.

Luis: Nah. I don't even know if they'd want to go.

Dad: The only way to find out is to invite them. Come on, I won't embarrass you, and this will give me a chance to know your friends better. The better I know your friends, the more comfortable I will be with you spending time with them.

Luis: Alright. I'll call them. But, you promise not to embarrass me?

Dad: I promise.

Parents want their children to have friends. Friends bring much joy to our lives, and we all want children to experience the fun, trust, and safety that come with having good friends. Parents start encouraging friendships for their children as soon as their children can sit-up. They are thrilled when their children learn to share, and they are proud when their children begin to speak and communicate with other children. Friendships allow children to experience the world outside of the home as they learn how to interact and share with non-family members. Friendships become more important to children as they get older. When children enter adolescence, their friendships can feel more important to them than any other relationship.

ENCOURAGE FRIENDSHIPS

Mother: Jeremiah, why don't you invite Zachary to go to the movies? You have been sitting in the house all summer.

Jeremiah: Nah. I'd rather just stay home.

Mother: Jeremiah, it is important to spend time with friends. It gives you someone else to do things with and talk to other than your family. I think you would really enjoy going to a movie with Zachary. Come on. I'll even give you money for popcorn.

Jeremiah: Alright. I'll call him.

Friendships need to be encouraged with children. Children who have friends feel a sense of belonging in school, and they have someone with whom to share activities outside of the family. Friends provide children with confidantes, laughter, activities and support. Friends help each other with homework, difficult situations, and celebrations. Friends help children feel valued and noticed. Children with friends are less likely to be bullied or harassed in school. They will have a more positive attitude towards life, and they will be motivated to do better in school. Children who have friends in school want to be in school. They look forward to going to school each day to be with their friends. Children who do not make friends in school will find attending school a struggle, as they feel excluded and lonely. Encourage your child to develop friendships with classmates or neighborhood children. Open up your home to your child's friends, and make it a place where they can gather and play. If your child is unsuccessful with making friends in school or in the neighborhood, find a club or hobby in which your child might be interested so that he or she can meet children with similar interests. Some children thrive on many friendships while others are content with one or two strong friendships. Allow your child the freedom to determine how many friends he or she is comfortable with developing. If your child has no interest in maintaining friendships and prefers to be alone, spend time with your child to determine if your child is sadder than usual. Consult with a professional if you are concerned about your child's behavior and lack of interest in forming relationships.

PEER INFLUENCE

Melinda: What are you doing?!

Valerie: I'm just letting the school know what I think of it.

Melinda: Valerie, you can't spray paint the walls. You'll get into trouble.

Valerie: Come on, Mel. It is not that big of deal. Now are you going to help me, or am I going to have to tell everyone what a loser you are?

Friends are an important part of childhood because they help children learn how to be in relationships and feel valued. Friends, though, can also influence children to make unhealthy choices. Many children find themselves in trouble because they succumbed to peer pressure. Too many children find themselves participating in vandalism, alcohol/drug abuse, skipping school or harassing another student because their friends encourage them to go against their better judgment. If your child is secretive about his or her friendships, this might be cause for concern. Your child might be spending time with children of whom you would not approve. Children who only have friends that are much older may also be involved in unhealthy activities such as drugs or gangs. Children might know that an action is wrong, but their desire to be accepted by their friends is stronger than their desire to do what is right.

All children, unfortunately, are not the best choices for friends. Some children do not have the home environment or personal skills needed to make good choices and be good friends. These children do need help, but they are not the best people with whom your child should be making friends. Children are not always the best judges of character. Teach your child traits that are important in friendships including respect, trust, and character. Talk about why having a friend who constantly gets into trouble either in school or with the police would be difficult, and compare it with having a friend who is happy and well-adjusted. Be clear with your child about what traits you are comfortable with in a friend.

Children will give in to peer pressure at times and make mistakes. This is a part of growing-up and learning about choices and consequences. Children, though, who continually give in to peer pressure and make unhealthy choices are in need of help. Children who have low self-esteem and/or are struggling with a personal issue are more likely to be influenced by peer pressure. These children are sending a message to the adults in their lives that they need help; they just do not know how to ask for it. If your child continually gets into trouble because of his or her friends, take action and consult with your child's school counselor for guidance. The sooner you help your child resolve his or her problems, the easier it will be to help your child make better choices.

KNOW FRIENDS AND THEIR PARENTS

Mother: Where are you going Leslie?

Leslie: To a friend's house.

Mother: Who is your friend?

Leslie: Some girl from school.

Mother: Does she have a name?

Leslie: Geez, Mom, why do you have to know everything?

Mother: I want to know who you are spending time with.

Leslie: Her name is Roberta, alright?!

Mother: Great. I will drive you to Roberta's house so I can meet her and her parents.

Leslie: Mom, I can go by myself.

Mother: I know you can go by yourself, but I want to know who it is you spend time with. I want to be sure Roberta's house is a place I am comfortable with. I want to know her parents. Your other option is to stay here with me and help me with laundry.

Leslie: (irritated) Alright. But hurry. She's waiting for me.

Parents need to know the friends of their children. When your child has a friend with whom he or she wants to spend time, invite the friend to your house and get to know him or her. Visit with the friend and listen to your instinct regarding the appropriateness of the friendship. Do not make a quick judgment based on appearance. Spend time getting to know your child's friend before deciding if he or she is a good match for your child. If you are not comfortable with your child's friend and you try to end the friendship, this might cause your child to assert his or her independence by wanting to keep the friendship despite your objections. Instead, be cautious of friends that are questionable, and closely monitor your child's activities with the friend. Do not comment positively or negatively about the person, but discuss the consequences of specific positive and negative qualities that can be found in friends. Give your child a chance to realize on his or her own that this friend is not a good match. If you decide that you must end one of your child's friendships, be prepared to closely monitor your child's activities so you know with whom he or she is spending time. Additionally, contact your child's school for assistance in keeping the children separated while at school. The best way to help your child choose the best friends with whom to spend time is to maintain a close relationship with your child. Your child will be more open to discussing friendships with you and seeking guidance if you maintain a close relationship with your child.

If your child wants to go to a friend's house, make it a point to meet the parents of the new friend. Feel free to ask the parents the following questions.

- Which adults will be supervising the children when my child is visiting?
- Who else is going to be in the house when my child is visiting?
- Are there guns in the house?
- What kinds of activities will the children be doing at the house?

Do not worry about offending the parents because you are entrusting your child in their care. Your child's safety should be a priority. The parents of your child's friends should be asking you the same questions when they allow their child to play at your house. You might even form your own friendships with the parents of your child's friends, which will create more security for your child.

Making and developing good friendships is an essential part of childhood. Your child is dependent on you to teach him or her how to be a friend and to learn about the important qualities of a friendship. Your child also needs you to help him or her make good choices about the type of person with whom he or she should be friends and ensuring that your child is safe when spending time with a friend away from home. Do not be shy about learning about your child's friends. Children can be powerful influences over their friends in school and at home. Parents need to know who their children's friends are and about the friends' families. Parents need to know with whom their children spend time when not at home. Although children might want their friendships to be separate from their family relationships, they still need the guidance and structure that only parents can provide.

17

Monitor Technology

Sherry is relieved to have a son who is so easy to parent. She never has to worry about Daniel staying out late, getting involved with drugs, or running with the "wrong crowd." Daniel is happy being at home with her and playing on the Internet. He often sits at the computer for hours each evening, and Sherry is glad that Daniel has a hobby he enjoys so much.

Technology has brought about tremendous strides in our ability to learn about the world. Television, the Internet, video games, cell phones, movies and music have changed the way we view society. We are able to learn about cultures in other countries, meet someone in a different state, and call someone from anywhere our cell phone signal will reach. We can shop, watch movies, listen to music on demand, and play with video games within the comforts of our home. Yet, just as technology has brought improvements into our daily life, it has also created problems that were unheard of twenty years ago.

We are a generation split by technology. As adults, our knowledge of technology ranges from being aware that it exists to being able to write software and program computers. Most adults fall somewhere in the middle of understanding technology. Children, though, are raised on technology. They are exposed to computers as babies, and much of their learning in school involves some kind of computer interaction. They are not afraid of technology. They are hungry to learn all they can about its potential. Consequently, our children know more than we do about technology, and many parents accept their own ignorance and are willing to be uninvolved in this area of their children's lives. As a result, children are exploring the limits of technology and finding themselves in difficult, if not dangerous, situations.

TELEVISION, MOVIES AND MUSIC

Ed loves watching action movies. He is amazed at how powerful and brave the characters are, and he stays glued to the television so he won't miss a fight. He fantasizes about how he will beat up any students at school who mess with him. They had better watch out because he knows how to fight like the guys in the movies.

Children typically watch several hours of television or videos each day with much of the programming containing violence. Children are becoming immune to seeing violent and brutal acts, and they are becoming more aggressive. They often imitate what they see on television, which leads to violence in the schools. The concerns about violence in the media have been around for many years. Studies have shown that children are affected by the sex and violence found in television programs (including cartoons), movies and music lyrics. The studies are clear that children who watch programs with violence or listen to music with violent lyrics have a greater likelihood of developing aggressive and anti-social characteristics. Children who watch violent programming and listen to music with violent lyrics are more likely to have a difficult time behaving appropriately at home and in school. This will, consequently, affect their ability to be successful. Parents must be aware of the programs, movies and music to which their children are being exposed. Parents cannot allow their children—including teenagers—to watch or listen to whatever is available. If you have pornographic videos hidden in your home, your child probably knows where they are, and he or she might have viewed them. Viewing pornography can distort a child's perception of healthy sexual relationships. Be aware of the dangers of keeping pornographic videos in your home. Children need to be protected from the violence and sex shown in the media for their own well-being.

Protect your child from unnecessary exposure to violence. Preview the programs, movies and music to which your child is exposed, or watch these programs and listen to the music with your child. If situations of violence occur, talk to your child about the difference between real and make-believe. Help your child to understand that the actors on the programs are not actually killed, and if the situation were to occur in real life, the person would be hurt or killed. Limit the amount of time you allow your child to watch television. Children who watch a lot of television are at risk for earning lower grades, reading less, being less active and becoming overweight. Discuss with your child the song lyrics that contain violence, and explain your beliefs regarding right and wrong. Actively monitor your child's exposure to violence through the media to guide your child's healthy development. For further information on violence in the media, you can visit www.parentstv.org.

VIDEO GAMES

Jamal cannot get his daughter to turn off the computer. She gets on it as soon as she comes home, and she rushes through dinner so that she can go back to playing her games. She never wants to go anywhere with the family anymore, and she never spends time outside playing. Jamal is beginning to wonder if her behavior is healthy.

Violence and sex can also be found in video games. Children are affected by what they see in the video games they are playing on television or on the computer. Watch your child play video games so that you are aware of what he or she is viewing.

Another danger in playing video games is the addiction that develops with some children. Even if the games seem to be harmless, children who spend several hours a day playing the games are at-risk to becoming addicted and getting lost in a fantasy world. An addiction is serious whether it is to drugs, food or computers. Children who become addicted to video games spend less time with their families and their grades fall as they spend less time studying and doing homework. As with a true addiction, children will not care about being successful in school or preparing for their future. All they can think about is isolating themselves and playing video games. If you are concerned about the amount of time your child is spending playing video games, take away his or her opportunities to play the games. Do not allow your child access to the computer except for completing homework under your supervision. If your child goes to a friend's house, be sure an adult will be there, and let the adult know that your child is not allowed to play video games. You may even have to notify your child's school so they can help monitor during school hours, and limit your child's access to restaurants that have computers for patrons. See how your child reacts for a few weeks. If your child becomes agitated, depressed, or begins sneaking out of the house, you may have a problem. Consult with a qualified professional for guidance. If your child does not seem to mind being away from the games, then you can allow him or her to begin playing with the games again, but limit the play time to thirty minutes a day. Playing on the computer longer than that can lead to structural changes in the brain and affect brain development. Addictions to video games can cause a decline in grades, depression, and isolation. Closely monitor the types of games your child is playing as well as the amount of time he or she spends on the computer.

INTERNET

Keisha could not wait to get home. She thought all day about what she was going to write to her chat room boyfriend, Anthony. She could not wait to tell him that she had been thinking about him all day, and she wanted to meet him. Keisha has never had a boyfriend and she feels so lucky to have met such a cool guy like Anthony on the Internet.

The Internet has transformed how society functions. Any information we want can be easily found by typing in the subject on a search engine and mountains of resources will appear. The Internet has also changed the way people communicate with each other and meet others. As with any type of technology, the Internet can be wonderful or devastating.

Parents of past generations were able to monitor to whom their children were talking by overhearing telephone conversations or seeing the people interacting with their children. The evolution of the Internet has silenced audible communication between children and others. Parents can no longer observe whom their children are visiting or listen to the conversations because the communication occurs through typed words and symbols. This has made monitoring a child's safety with others more of a challenge. Yet, as past generations of parents learned how to handle the challenges of their day, parents today can become just as skilled with monitoring technology.

Parents have the vital role of protecting their children from much of the information that is available on the Web. Sites related to pornography, violence and questionable topics can be filtered by parents. Children will be exposed to many questionable sites if filters are not used, as children are easy targets. Using software designed to protect children while they are online is a good start to keeping inappropriate material away from children. There are many different types of parental control software available.

- Filtering software works to prevent inappropriate content from appearing on your computer. These programs use certain criteria to determine whether or not a website will be allowed to be viewed on the computer. This type of software can also prevent certain private information from being shared on the Internet such as your children's names and telephone numbers.
- Blocking software uses a list of websites that are not allowed to be viewed on the computer, and/or it can have a list of limited websites that are only allowed to be viewed on the computer.
- Monitoring or tracking software gives parents an extra set of eyes to know what their children are viewing on the computer.
- Keylogger programs are some of the most comprehensive software programs that parents can use. These programs record every keystroke made on the computer. Information can be retrieved by parents to see what children have been typing online.

Most of the software on the market designed to protect children while they are on the computer does a fairly good job. Ask for recommendations, though, from your children's school's computer specialist or librarian, or research recommendations on the Internet. Services are also available through your Internet Service Provider. Regardless of what you use for protection, remember that nothing is foolproof. The persistence of others who want to cause harm to children and/or the curiosity of young minds can sometimes fool even the best software.

Children are usually very comfortable with surfing the Internet. They know how to find research needed for school and learn about different topics that might interest them. Children's use of the Internet can be difficult for parents because parents often trust that their children are safe when they are on the computer, but their children may become victims of cyber predators. Children often participate in chat rooms, which are places that people can meet and get to know other people anywhere in the world. Chat rooms are usually not monitored, and there is no one that controls the appropriateness of the conversations. Chat rooms are considered to the one of the most dangerous areas on the Internet for potential sex abuse. Predators often go to chat rooms meant for children, and they pose as a child in order to communicate with another child. This is all done in an effort to have an illicit relationship with a child. There is no way of knowing if a person in a chat room is who the person says he or she is. Children have to be extremely cautious when entering a chat room site to ensure that they remain safe. Many adolescents have unknowingly agreed to meet a friend they talked to in a chat room, and these children discover that their friend is actually an adult. Some children have been abducted and/or assaulted as a result of meeting their chat room friends. Chat rooms should be considered a public place. There is no privacy in your home when your child is in a chat room. Discuss the dangers of chat rooms with your child, and closely monitor its use.

Instant Messaging, or IM, has become a popular way for people to communicate. IM differs slightly from chat rooms in that it is usually a conversation held on the Internet between two people—although group conversations can occur. Children often engage in Instant Messaging while doing their homework on the computer. IM can be easily abused to spread rumors or gossip about someone. The precautions used for chat rooms should also be implemented when using Instant Messaging.

Another popular way for children to communicate online is through social networking sites. These sites offer users a web page to post their blogs, photographs, video clips and list interests and activities. They also provide opportunities for others to make comments about someone's webpage and try to contact the author of the webpage through email or instant messaging. Blogs are equivalent to the private journals people used to keep hidden under their mattresses. Children, now, keep their private thoughts in their blogs which they post online. Children usually do not understand that what they post online is not private—even if they limit its access to a few friends. Information found online can be forwarded, copied, and manipulated by another. Social networking sites also contain videos that are posted online. People can make home videos to share with others through their sites or use websites created for video-sharing. This is another creative outlet for children, but many cautions should be used to keep the identities of children safe.

Social networking sites must be monitored by parents. Parents should periodically read their children's webpages to be sure that everything posted is appropriate and safe. Parents are often concerned about invading their children's privacy by reading the webpages, but the Internet is not private. Others are reading the webpages, and parents need to be a part of the audience as well. If children want to keep a private journal, then they can be provided with a notebook for their thoughts that they can keep in their rooms.

Adolescents enjoy social networking sites because they can express themselves and try on different personalities. The practice of writing and expressing oneself is a good activity for children, but children often do not have good judgment to determine what material is appropriate and safe. The webpages found on these sites are very appealing to predators. There is so much identifiable information given by children that it is easy for predators to start a relationship with an unsuspecting child and eventually arrange for a meeting. Children will often share names, school names, hometowns, cell phone numbers and email addresses on their web pages. Parents have a responsibility to view their children's web pages to ensure that no identifiable information is shared.

An emerging interactive activity for children is online gaming. Children used to play video games alone with a computer. If they wanted company while playing, they would invite a friend over or talk to a friend on the speakerphone while playing the game. Recent advances in technology have opened the door for children to play video games with a group of others from around the world. The interactive games use headsets and microphones so players can talk to each other live while playing the game. The "voice chat" might start out harmless, but as the games become intense, players often use obscene language and/or bully other players. Internet predators can also join the games in an attempt to meet young children. The ability to talk to others through computers using microphones and headsets allows predators unlimited access to children who are playing games. Children are usually not as guarded when playing a game, and they might be more willing to give out personal information such as emails or telephone numbers while on voice chat. Children can be easily persuaded to give out phone numbers since they reason that talking through voice chat and talking on the telephone is the same thing. Voice chat is not the same thing as talking on the telephone. Children cannot be traced through voice chat, but if they give out their telephone numbers, an address can be easily located through the Internet. Children must be educated about the dangers that can occur with interactive gaming. Some games offer voice masks so that children's voices will be distorted making it more difficult to identify their ages and genders. Some games also offer reporting procedures if the game participants become too vulgar or obscene. But, many games do not have safety features built in and they pose a risk for children—especially inexperienced gamers. Parents must closely monitor their children's participation in online gaming until the children show they are mature enough to handle the challenges that might surface while playing games. Children can be taught the following safety measures to take when participating in online gaming.

- You have the right to leave the game if the conversation becomes uncomfortable or offensive.
- Stop talking to any player who is asking inappropriate questions or who is requesting personal information.
- Always tell a parent when a player is behaving inappropriately or is trying to get personal information. The parent can help the child report the incident.

Online gaming can be a fun activity for children, but it does need to be monitored, and children must be taught safety rules for participating in the games.

The Internet also presents risks for children who are enticed into becoming involved with illegal activities. There are numerous sites that allow people to purchase guns, gamble, purchase drugs, learn how to make bombs, promote hate, and offer numerous other illegal or questionable activities or beliefs. The Internet is an open door for any enterprise or thought that one person wants to share with the world. Children often do not have the maturity to make good choices when exposed to these sites. Parental control software will help you monitor to what your child is exposed so that you can allow your child to explore the Internet without fear of encountering objectionable websites. Yet, even if you utilize the safety software, you must continue to be diligent about monitoring your child's surfing activities to ensure that he or she remains protected.

Downloading music, videos, and other files is popular with children using P2P (peer-to-peer) software. This software can be downloaded onto your computer, and files can be shared between computers. People are able to share files that belong to others or share with each other files that are "homemade." The problem with downloading shared files is that copyright laws are frequently violated, and children and parents can be sued for copyright infringement. Educate your children about what it means to violate copyright laws, and monitor your children's sharing of materials.

Children are also at risk for being exposed to pornography through the Internet. It is very easy for children to have access to pornographic material on the Internet. Even if parents are periodically monitoring what their children are viewing, children can quickly change screens to keep what they are really looking at hidden from their parents. Additionally, the Internet is filled with people trying to promote pornography to children. Children are easy targets on which to make money or exploit. Many parents would be shocked to learn about the amount of pornography to which their children are exposed. In addition to the developmental concerns of children viewing pornography, children's perception of what is normal for sexuality is severely distorted when they see pornography. This can lead to difficulties in establishing healthy sexual relationships in later years. Talk to a computer expert at your child's school to learn how to block websites from your computer and monitor the websites your child has been visiting for your child's protection.

Many businesses, such as bookstores and coffee houses, now offer wireless Internet access (Wi-Fi) where someone can take their laptop and connect to the Internet. This can potentially allow children unmonitored access to the Internet. Cards are also available to use in laptops where the Internet can be accessed anywhere if the user subscribes to a service that provides a signal. Additionally, the Internet can be accessed through cell phones, portable media players, PDAs, video games and other portable devices. Consequently, teaching children how to keep themselves safe online is an essential part of parenting.

Despite concerns related to children using the Internet, it is a valuable source of educational material. Your child does need to have access to a computer for schoolwork and learning opportunities. Yet, as the parent, you need to monitor its use. If you do not understand about the Internet or how to use the computer, contact your school for information on computer courses. The more you know, the better equipped you will be to monitor your child's use of the computer. You must be actively involved in knowing what your child is viewing on the computer. The following tips will help you monitor your child and keep him or her safe:

- Keep the computer in a common room in the house, i.e. the

family room. Do not allow your child to be on the computer alone in the bedroom. If your child has a laptop computer with wireless capability, be aware of when and where your child uses the computer.

- Talk to your child about the dangers of the Internet--especially participating in chat rooms. Encourage your child to tell you about his or her experiences on the Internet.
- Frequently check the Web history on your computer to see what sites your child has visited. If you do not know how to do this, ask an expert.
- Share an email account with your child so you know who is emailing your child.
- Monitor your credit cards bills, and look for unexpected charges.
- Teach your child to not give out any personal information on the Internet including name, age, email address, telephone number, home address, and school name. Have your child use a fake name if needed.
- Never allow your child to have a face-to-face meeting with anyone that he or she has met on the Internet.
- Limit the amount of time your child spends on the Internet. The Internet can become an addiction, and this can affect your child's academic progress as well as family relationships.
- Be aware of changes in your child's behavior, which could be related to Internet activity.
- Install software such as Net Nanny, Cybersitter, or Eblaster that will limit the sites available to your child.
- Closely monitor your child's use of a webcam if your computer has one. A webcam allows images to be shared through the Internet. This feature can easily be abused by predators who contact your child and convince him or her to use the webcam for illicit purposes.

CELL PHONES

Marissa: Call me tonight.

Pat: How late can I call?

Marissa: It doesn't matter. Call me on my cell. My parents never know when I get calls on my cell.

Cell phones are everywhere these days. Their use is no longer limited to people in business. Children, college students, parents and grandparents all have access to cell phones. Cell phones are excellent to have in case of an emergency or to stay connected with a family member. Many families have chosen to give their children their own cell phones to use in place of the home phone. Consequently, some schools have had to ban cell phone use during the school day because they are too distracting. The choice to give children cell phones is a personal choice made by parents, but their use should be closely monitored.

Adolescents can use cell phones to do more than talk to family or friends.

- Students use cell phones to play games—often during class time.
- Other children use cell phones to stay in contact with forbidden boyfriends or girlfriends. Children can give their cell phone numbers to anyone and receive calls from people of whom their parents are unaware.
- Cell phones can be used to take pictures of others without their permission, i.e. in locker rooms.
- Illegal activities such as drug dealing or gambling can be conducted through cell phones.
- The Internet can be accessed through the cell phones allowing for unsupervised chat room conversations or emails.
- People can text message each other on cell phones. Text messaging evolved as a response to the time it takes to type a message on a telephone keypad. Complete words or sentences are not used. Everything is abbreviated or substituted. A huge communication gap is occurring as children understand the language of text messaging, but parents are clueless. This can become dangerous when parents do not understand the messages their children are sending

through the cell phones. Children can unknowingly make themselves vulnerable to identity thieves, predators and cyberbullies. Log on to www.webopedia.com/quick_ref/text messageabbreviations.asp for a helpful reference guide on text messaging translations.

For your child's safety:

- teach your child to never reveal any personal information through text messaging;
- do not post cell phone numbers online;
- never respond to text messaging from an unknown person; and
- never let a stranger use the cell phone.

New technology is helping parents monitor their children's cell phone use. New cell phone products feature a variety of parental controls including presetting which calls can be made from the phone and which calls can be received. Cell phone technology will continue to advance creating more concerns for children's safety but also providing more security features for kids. Parents' awareness of their children's cell phone activities is the best protection for children's safety.

Cell phones, like any technology, have great benefits, but they can also be abused. Monitor your child's cell phone use. Look at the phone numbers printed on the phone bill each month to note whom your child is dialing, who is calling your child, and what times the phone calls are occurring. If your child goes out for the evening, have him or her call you from a land phone so you can be sure from where he or she is calling. Do not allow your child to use the cell phone during school hours. It is tempting to play games, talk or text message others during school, but this is a distraction and it can affect learning. Consider putting away your child's cell phone when he or she is at home. If you have a house phone, your child can make and receive phone calls on the telephone at home, and it will be easier to monitor its use. Additionally, determine if your child really needs to take a cell phone when he or she is with the family at restaurants, the movies, shopping, at relatives' homes or other family activities. There should not be any type of emergency for your child that his or her friends must contact your child during family outings. Family time should be for the family without the intrusion of others. Your child can talk to friends when the family returns home. Lastly, impress upon your child to not use his or her cell phone when driving a car. Too many accidents occur when drivers are distracted by their cell phone conversations.

Parenting has always been difficult. The arrival of technology, though, has made the job even more of a challenge. Technology is an essential tool in your child's education, but it can also be a detriment to your child's learning and well-being. Parents often have concerns about their children's privacy rights when it comes to monitoring Internet and cell phone activities. The safety of children takes precedence over concerns about their privacy. The Internet is filled with adults who are intent on harming children. Additionally, the cyberbullying that occurs online is very damaging. Children are children. They do not have the same level of maturity or judgment as their parents. Children need their parents to be involved in technology so that children remain safe. Closely monitor your child's involvement in different types of technology, and if you are not sure of what you should be aware, talk to the technology coordinator in your child's school or another computer expert. The technology coordinator can provide you with a wealth of information on how to use technology to help your child succeed while monitoring it so that your child remains safe.

More information about online safety can be found at:

www.cyberbully.org
www.internetsuperheroes.org
www.i-safe.org
www.missingkids.com
www.netsmartz.org
www.safekids.com
www.safeteens.com
www.stopcyberbullying.org
www.surfswellisland.com
www.wiredsafety.org

18

Teach Tolerance

Chen hates going to school. He cannot think as quickly as other students, and some students make fun of him. He doesn't always understand what they are saying to him, but he understands what it means when they laugh at him. He trusts no one at school, because he never knows if they are going to be his friend or if they are going to make fun of him.

There was a time in our society where different groups of people did not mix. When my father was growing up in Poth, Texas in the 1930's, the immigrants from Germany did not mix with the immigrants from Poland. It was quite a scandal in the small town if two people from different countries dated. The lines have blurred over time between some groups, but there is still discrimination in many aspects of society. One of the biggest challenges found in schools is to teach students to accept each other regardless of background, preferences, learning abilities, social maturity or appearance. Schools today have students that are a mixture of ethnic groups, accents, colors, genders, heights, weights, mannerisms, disabilities and financial status. It is not uncommon to find a school that has children of millionaires sitting next to children who live on dirt floors. Today's nutrition, eating and exercise habits and genetics have resulted in students of the same age having over six inches difference in height or one hundred pounds difference in weight. The gay rights movement has encouraged students who identify as gay or lesbian to be more open about their identities. Federal legislation from the 1970's mandates that all children be educated regardless of disabilities, so children of different physical, emotional and learning challenges are eligible to be in regular education classes depending on their abilities. Additionally, the constant flow of immigration has filled classrooms with students from around the world. The United States believes in a free education for all children, and our classrooms represent this belief. For this reason in itself, children must learn how to respect differences found in their fellow students, and this learning must begin at home.

Discrimination has always existed. There has always been and there always will be people who are treated differently based on background, appearance or abilities. Children learn how to discriminate or not discriminate by listening to and watching their parents. Parents are the primary teachers for showing their children how to treat other people. Children who enter school with a prejudice against a group of people will either get into trouble for discriminating against another student through words, actions or ignoring the student, or they will constantly be challenged to keep thoughts unspoken. Children who do discriminate can become instigators of bullying or harassment, and their actions can cause another student to feel ostracized in school. Our society has become so blended with different types of people that all students need to learn how to be tolerant of differences and treat all people with respect simply because they are people.

The Southern Poverty Law Center has a website at www.tolerance. org dedicated to promoting tolerance in an effort to end discrimination and create empathy through education. Their website lists ways to nurture tolerance in children. Lessons in tolerance begin in early childhood and continue until adulthood. Your child will learn from you about how all people are different but equal; how everyone should be treated with compassion and kindness; and how everyone has a purpose in our world. Look for teachable moments each day (found in books, movies, discussing experiences and/or observing others) to create a knowing in your child about tolerance and empathy for others and to expose your child to different world perspectives. These lessons will strengthen your child's character and build his or her foundation for success

You are your child's primary teacher on how to interact with the world. Your child watches how you treat others who are different from you and how you react when in the presence of discrimination. When you treat others with respect and courtesy, your child will learn to do the same. There are numerous teachable moments where you can reinforce the lessons you are teaching your child. If you see your child notice someone in public who looks different, use that opportunity to remind your child that no one is better or worse than the other; we are all just different. If your child makes a loud comment about someone's appearance in public, do not whisk your child away. Instead, remind your child that even though everyone has differences, we are all ultimately the same people. When your child hears comments that are discriminatory, talk to your child about why others make comments and how it feels to be the recipient of discrimination. Share your own stories of discrimination, and teach about significant times in history and today where people are treated differently. Maintain an open communication with your child about tolerance, and encourage your child to talk to you when he or she has questions about another person.

Find out what your child's school does to promote tolerance among the students. If no diversity program exists, meet with school officials to begin a program. When students are not educated about accepting others regardless of differences, it creates an atmosphere of bullying and rejection for students who are different from the mainstream. Students who are rejected or ridiculed can resort to violence against themselves or others in an attempt to be noticed and express their pain. All students should feel comfortable and welcomed in their school regardless of differences. The Southern Poverty Law Center website www.tolerance.org and the website for the National Conference for Community and Justice www.nccj.org both offer ideas for parents and schools on how to promote tolerance and equality among students.

Teaching your child tolerance will help him or her be more successful in school. Students who are accepting of others regardless of differences become the leaders of the school. These are the students who are not afraid to embrace an outcast or speak out for a ridiculed student. Tolerant students are the students whom others feel safe to be around because they know they are accepted regardless of differences. School officials notice the students that promote tolerance, and they invite them to take on leadership roles in the school because these students represent the attitude and character that all schools strive to promote. Help your child achieve success by learning how to positively interact with others and treat all students will dignity. This is a lesson that your child will successfully carry well into adulthood.

19

Model Healthy Eating and Exercise

Mother: My son won't eat. He has lost 20 pounds in the last three months. He says he is fat, and he needs to lose weight. But, he is too skinny, and I worry that he will keep losing weight.

Counselor: Why do you think he believes that he is fat?

Mother: Well, my husband is always making comments about my son's body telling him that he is flabby and that he will never make it as a football player with his body. He makes comments to me, too, about my weight. But, I've learned to ignore it. It really bothers my son, though.

Counselor: So, what message is your son getting about his body and his worth.

Mother: I know it sounds bad, and my son now worries that he is too fat to be a good athlete. But, that is not what my husband means. He is just trying to motivate him to be athletic.

Counselor: So, what is your husband teaching your son?

Mother: That he will not be a star football player like his father unless he loses weight.

Counselor: What else?

Mother: I guess that he is not good enough like he is.

Our society is obsessed with body image. Adults and children are striving for the perfect body that does not exist. Children are watching television, movies and the adults in their lives to learn what their bodies are supposed to look like and to learn how to get the perfect body. Children have learned to use food to cope with problems and emotions by either eating too much or eating too little. Children are teased and treated as outcast if they do not have an acceptable body. The obsession with bodies and food is causing children to struggle with participating in everyday activities, social relationships and school. They are constantly receiving messages about their bodies through the media, peers, and family members. Most of the messages say that thinner is better. Eating disorders are affecting younger children causing elementary aged children to obsess about food and bodies. Children are using food or avoiding food as a way of coping with emotions. This is leading to an unprecedented number of children becoming anorexic, bulimic or compulsive overeaters.

ANOREXIA

Angie looks in the mirror, and she sees fat hanging on her body. When she doesn't eat, she knows she is getting rid of the fat. Angie feels so good when she doesn't eat. She is in control. She is always tired and cold, and she cannot concentrate in school, but she doesn't care. She just wants to be thin.

I work with many young girls and boys who refuse to eat because they believe that they are fat. These children may not be diagnosed as having anorexia, but they adopting dangerous eating habits in an effort to be thin. If their habits continue, they are at risk for becoming anorexic. Children diagnosed with anorexia have a fear of being fat even though they are underweight. When these children look into the mirror, they do not see their bodies as they actually are; they see bodies full of fat. Children with anorexia may show the following signs:
- underweight;
- fear of gaining weight;
- distorted perception of body;

- withdrawing from family and friends;
- wearing baggy clothing;
- mood changes;
- secretiveness; and/or
- unusual behavior including anxiety around meals.

If a child is exhibiting symptoms of anorexia—especially severe weight loss—a consultation with a health care provider is recommended for guidance. The child will probably resist efforts for help, but his or her life could be in danger. Children who suffer from anorexia are struggling more with emotions than food. They are refraining from food and starving themselves as a way of coping with overwhelming emotions. Children with anorexia generally need a combination of medical treatment and emotional therapy to help them learn how to cope with their emotions and develop healthy lifestyles. For more information about anorexia, consult with your health care provider or contact the Eating Disorders Association website at www.edauk.com.

BULIMIA NERVOSA

Malaya obsesses with food. She thinks about it all day in school. She fantasizes about what she will eat when she gets home. She imagines the sensation of biting into a candy bar, and then eating the cookies hidden in her drawer. She knows she will throw-up everything she eats, but she does not think about that right now. She had promised herself that she would not do this anymore, but she will just do it one more day. Tomorrow, she will stop binging and purging.

Children with bulimia eat a lot of food in a short time period and then force themselves to vomit, exercise excessively, and/or take laxatives, diuretics or enemas. Children with bulimia, like anorexics, are obsessed with their body image, but they eat uncontrollably and then get rid of the food typically by vomiting. Bulimics generally are of normal weight, but their bodies show physical signs of maltreatment. Signs of bulimia nervosa include:

- mood changes;

- abdominal problems such as constipation and bloating;
- tooth decay;
- throat problems;
- irregular heartbeat;
- physically weak;
- unhealthy looking skin and hair loss;
- obsession with food;
- excessive exercise;
- secretive behavior; and/or
- death.

Children who suffer from bulimia are coping with their emotional problems through overeating. Their resulting fear of gaining weight leads them to vomit and/or use medication to rid their bodies of the food. It is harder to detect children who are bulimic because their body weight does not drastically change. Yet, these children give other signs such as problems with skin and teeth, secretive behavior, and large amounts of food missing from the home or food hidden in the home. Children who suffer from bulimia nervosa are generally resistant to help because this is the only way they know how to cope with their emotions. They eat to cope, and then their overwhelming fear of gaining weight causes them to purge themselves of the calories they ingest during a binge. These children, though, need medical help because they are endangering their health. They also need counseling in order to learn healthier ways of coping with their emotions. For more information about bulimia nervosa, consult with your health care provider or contact the Eating Disorders Association website at www.edauk.com.

COMPULSIVE EATING

Misha is uncomfortable in his body. He does not fit into the school desks, and he hates going to P.E. class. The other students make fun of him all of the time. He laughs with them because he does not want them to see his feelings are hurt. Instead, he goes home everyday, sits in front of the television, and eats until he feels sick.

Children come in all body types, and some children will tend to be heavier than others. Obesity, though, occurs when children weigh significantly more than the recommended range for their height and body type. Children often mimic their parents' behavior when it comes to diet and exercise, so if a parent is overweight, the child is more likely to be overweight. Obesity in children, though, can lead to health problems as well as social isolation. Children often become obese through compulsive eating which can be triggered by emotional difficulties.

Children who compulsively overeat tend to be heavier than their peers, and they are excluded from activities. The need to overeat is often the result of needing to cope with overwhelming emotions, and overeating numbs the child so he or she does not feel emotional pain. Ironically, the more a child tries to numb emotional pain through food, the more weight he or she gains. The resulting weight gain can lead to more problems including:

- feelings of shame and embarrassment;
- being a victim of bullying and teasing;
- few friends;
- limited involvement in activities;
- low self-esteem;
- depression or other emotional problems;
- breathing problems;
- trouble with bones and joints;
- lack of energy;
- diabetes; and/or
- difficulty sleeping.

Children who are overweight can be happy and well-adjusted, but their health is still a concern. Children can learn to lead a healthier lifestyle by following healthy examples set by their parents.

- Exercise daily.
- Involve the whole family in an active lifestyle that can include walks in the park or bicycling in the neighborhood. This is a great time to talk to children about what is occurring in their lives.

- Avoid fast food meals and cook healthy, low fat meals at home.
- Eat meals together as a family rather than in front of the television.
- Do not keep high sugar foods in the house such as candy and cookies.
- Focus on developing healthy diet and exercise habits rather than body weight.
- Do not make negative comments about own body, child's body or someone else's body.
- Let children know that their value lies in who they are rather than body weight. Encourage children to talk if they are being teased because of weight.
- Communicate with children about their fears, concerns and problems. Teach children to talk, journal, draw or exercise as a way of coping with emotions rather than eating.

A change in the family lifestyle will often help children lose weight. Children can be encouraged to be active by participating in athletics or another group activity. A school counselor or another professional can work with children who are struggling with an eating disorder. There might be an emotional issue with which these children need help in coping so that they no longer need to use food to cope with emotions. For more information about compulsive eating, consult with your school counselor or health care provider or contact the Eating Disorders Association website at www.edauk.com.

Children who use food to handle emotions are endangering their health and limiting their success. Children who develop problems with eating are at-risk for a variety of problems including social isolation, depression and school difficulties. Teaching children healthy ways of coping with emotions and living a healthy lifestyle can be challenge, but the most powerful teacher is modeling. You can show your child how to eat healthy and live an active lifestyle through your own habits. You can also teach your child healthy ways of handling emotions by talking about situations and feelings that your child is experiencing and giving your child the support and empathy that he or she needs to make healthy choices. An excellent children's book that teaches acceptance of different body types is *Shapesville* by Andy Mills and Becky Osborn. Read and discuss this book or similar books with your child to help build a healthy body image. Children who learn from their parents that they can talk to others to help resolve feelings and that their value does not lie in their body shape will have a greater chance of living a healthy lifestyle and finding success.

20

Stay Connected to Your Child's Emotional Health

Lester seems to be a happy child. He spends a lot of time with his family, and he is an A/B student. He plays football, and he loves to watch TV. Lately, though, he has been making comments about killing himself. His parents are surprised at these comments, but they do not believe that a nine-year old boy would be serious about killing himself. They decide not to worry about the comments, and to just try to continue creating a good life for Lester.

The emotional health of children is a frightening topic for parents. All parents want their children to be happy, but many parents do not know what to do or how to react when their children begin showing signs of emotional distress. Adolescence is a time of varied moods and emotions, so it can be difficult to judge if your child is going through a normal adolescent phase or if your child is in need of help. Staying connected with your child and maintaining good communication is a vital part of keeping your child safe and healthy. Many factors contribute to emotional problems in childhood. Some of the factors can be controlled and some of them cannot be prevented. Fac-

133

tors such as child abuse, a parent who abuses substances, a parent who is always working, or problems in school can be reduced or eliminated by a parent who decides that the health and well-being of his or her child is more important than the activity that is causing the child distress. Factors such as the death of a parent, moving to a new town, parental divorce, or a child's disability cannot be controlled, but children can be given the skills needed to cope with the stressful situations. When children are under stress or experiencing emotional difficulties, they need to be given the support and tools required to successfully work through their problems. When children are left alone to deal with their lives, the problems can become overwhelming. Children will handle problems the best they can, yet when the coping strategies that children use no longer work, they can begin to see unhealthy behaviors such as drug use or suicide as the only options. When parents and other adults are connected to children, much of the emotional distress and confusion that children experience can be managed.

SELF ESTEEM

Helen does not believe that anyone cares about her. She cannot see why anyone would want to be her friend. She is fat and ugly, and she never knows what to say to people. Helen is lonely, and she wishes that she were pretty and popular like the other girls so that she would have friends.

A healthy self-esteem gives children the strength needed to become emotionally healthy adults. Self-esteem consists of the beliefs, attitudes and feelings that people have about themselves which they use to find their place in the world. The development of a healthy self-esteem begins at birth. The response that parents have towards their babies' cries teaches the babies whether or not the world is a trustworthy place. As children develop, their interactions with others show children whether or not they matter to the world. Children who live with criticism and abuse will learn that they are not good enough. Children learn to believe that they deserve to be treated badly, and the world is not a good place. Children who grow up with positive praise and support learn that they have the resources needed to be successful. Even if these children encounter difficult times, they have the confidence to endure the difficulties and emerge stronger.

Children's self-esteems become stronger each time they experience success and make choices for themselves. Children who experience success while growing up develop a healthy self-esteem. Children need to be given opportunities to be successful with a variety of tasks such as picking up toys or reading a book. It is healthy for children to experience failure, but ultimately, they need to eventually find success in activities. Children who learn how to make choices for themselves develop a healthy self-esteem. Children who are allowed to choose between two shirts or choose what books to read learn that they have the ability to navigate in the world. Children who give up easily with tasks, who are not allowed the opportunities to make choices, and/or who are frequently criticized or berated by others may develop a low self-esteem. They begin believing that they are worthless and unable to achieve success. Children will develop healthy self-esteems if they have positive interactions with others that consist of praise and support, they are allowed to make choices for themselves, and they have opportunities to experience success.

Parents are crucial in helping their children develop a healthy self-esteem, and this can be accomplished through a variety of ways.

- Parents need to be aware of the words they choose when talking to their children. Children thrive on parents' praise and encouragement. Children who grow up hearing their parents tell them they are wonderful, smart, creative and capable grow to believe that they can accomplish anything. Praises like this are gold to children. Likewise, children who grow up hearing that they are stupid, ugly, useless or a mistake learn that they do not have the resources needed to be successful, and they believe that they are failures.

- When children make negative comments themselves, those comments should be countered with something positive. If children comment that they are stupid, give instances where smart choices were made. When children fail at a task, remind them that it is okay to fail, and they will eventually succeed.

- Parents are their children's role models. Parents need to treat themselves and others in their home with respect and positive praise. Remarks or criticisms about a parent's failure or the failure of someone else should be avoided. When children see that parents believe in their own worthiness, the children will believe in their own worthiness as well.
- Children need positive and concrete feedback about activities and tasks such as, "I know you are angry with your sister, but I am proud of you for not calling her names. Let's talk to your sister about what happened so that you can keep playing together."
- Children will benefit from being involved with volunteer activities or group activities where they can experience success. Successful experiences reinforce children's view of themselves as capable and important.
- The home must be a safe and nurturing environment for children. The home should be one where children can relax and be comfortable.

Parents play a vital role in helping their children develop a healthy self-esteem. All children will experience challenging times, but children who have a healthy and positive sense of who they are will more likely become stronger as a result of the challenges. This strength will lead to success in school and life.

STRESS

Alicia is considered the perfect student by her teachers. She is in all honors classes and makes all A's. She is always respectful, and she volunteers for several activities at school. Additionally, Alicia helps her mother take care of the three younger siblings at home, and she helps her mother with the cooking and cleaning. Alicia, though, is often tired, and she feels overwhelmed with her life. But, she is determined to not let anyone down. She does not want to disappoint her teachers or her mother, so she works hard to be the kind of person she thinks they want her to be.

Children experience stress. Some children experience more stress than others, and some children handle stress better than others. Many parents are surprised to learn that their children are under stress. A common thought is, "You don't have to worry about working or paying bills. All you have to do is go to school and learn. How stressful can that be?" Yet, children have more things occurring in their lives than learning in school. Stressful situations for children can include:

- academic demands of school;
- family problems including divorce, fighting, chronic illness and finances;
- negative thoughts or feelings about self;
- feeling pressured to look, behave or dress a certain way;
- living in an unsafe home, neighborhood or school;
- normal hormonal changes in body;
- problems with friends or peers;
- death of a loved one;
- moving;
- overly involved in activities; and/or
- physical and/or learning difficulties.

Stress can be overwhelming for some children leading them to unhealthy behaviors. Stress factors can trigger a child to cope with the ensuing overwhelming feelings by turning to alcohol, drugs, food, and/or delinquent activities. Children who are stressed can neglect school, sleep too much or too little, complain of physical ailments and have a change in mood or behavior. Stress in children, though, can be managed.

Parents can help children manage stress by staying connected with their children. Talk to your child about his or her concerns, fears and anxieties. Ask your child what causes children to feel overwhelmed or pressured, and ask your child if he or she is experiencing any of the pressures. Learn and teach techniques to help your child develop coping skills to alleviate the pressure that he or she feels. Monitor your child's activities, and do not allow your child to become overly involved. Children often do not have the maturity to set limits for themselves, and they depend on the adults in their lives for guidance.

If your child experiences a stressful event such as the death of a family member or pet or changing schools, talk frequently with your child about the experience and closely monitor his or her mood. Consult with the school counselor if you are worried about your child's well being.

Children can learn how to manage stress. You can teach your child stress reducing skills, and model these skills for your child. Stress management includes the following techniques.

- Exercise regularly and eat a healthy diet.
- Practice relaxation exercises such as steady breathing and relaxing muscles.
- Be aware of negative self-talk and work to replace it with positive thoughts.
- Develop healthy friendships.
- Spend time each day in relaxing activities such as listening to music, drawing or walking a dog.
- Talk to an adult when feeling overwhelmed.
- Avoid substance abuse.

Children who learn how to manage stress at an early age will be better prepared for the challenges of adolescence as they get older.

DEPRESSION

Andrew doesn't care anymore about school or friends. He used to be active and popular in school, but none of that matters anymore. Ever since his mom died last year, things have not been right. Andrew tries to be happy so that his dad does not worry about him, but he just can't do it anymore. All he wants to do is stay in his room.

Children do suffer from depression. The signs of depression are occurring more frequently in children of all ages. Children who are under stress are at a higher risk for developing symptoms of depression. Since there are more factors in today's society that are causing children to experience stress, more children today are showing signs of depression. Parents need to be aware of the signs of depression and seek help if they are concerned about their child. Common signs of depression in children include:

- often sad and/or crying;
- feeling hopeless, apathetic, and/or feeling tired;
- frequently angry, irritable or frustrated;
- wanting to be alone;
- physical complaints;
- failing grades;
- feelings of worthlessness or guilt;
- difficulties with concentrating or paying attention;
- change in eating or sleeping habits;
- expressing suicidal thoughts or desire to run away;
- withdrawing from activities;
- abusing alcohol or drugs; and/or
- behavior problems at home and/or in school.

Talk to your school counselor, health care provider or another professional if your child is persistently exhibiting any of these symptoms. Signs of depression in children should be taken seriously. If left untreated, children can fall further into making unhealthy choices including substance abuse, running away or suicide. Children who are depressed suffer in their academics, social relationships, and health. Depression can occur in all children regardless of ethnicity, financial status or gender. Feelings of depression increase the risk for suicide, so a professional should evaluate a child who is experiencing these feelings to determine the most appropriate intervention.

You can help your child find healthy ways of identifying and coping with emotions. Children often are not taught to identify the wide range of emotions that they experience while growing-up. Most children can identify commonly known emotions such as angry, sad or happy. Yet, they are limited in their vocabulary when asked to identify other emotions that they might experience, such as confused, frustrated or shocked. Ask your school counselor or librarian to recommend a book or poster about emotions, and talk to your child about what each emotion means. Ask him or her to tell about a time when he or she felt that way. Ask your child to draw what each emotion looks like.

As your child improves his or her skills in identifying emotions, he or she will be more likely to talk to you about feelings that he or she experiences rather than keeping them hidden and feeling depressed. You can also teach your child to express emotions in a variety of ways including journaling, arts and crafts and exercise. Children can cope with the emotions they experience during adolescence, but they need someone to teach them the skills needed to cope in healthy ways.

SELF-INJURY

All Mina can think about is cutting her arm. She is trying to stop, but she had an argument with her boyfriend, and she needs to cut to feel better. She feels ashamed every time she cuts, and she knows her parents would be mad if they found out about it. But, if she doesn't cut, she feels like she will go crazy.

Self-injury occurs when a person purposely hurts him or herself in an effort to cope with intense emotions. The types of self-injury can include burning self, hitting self with objects or fists, picking at scabs so that sores don't heal, chewing on the inside of the cheek, cutting skin or a host of other acts whose purpose is to inflict pain. (Some people who have multiple body piercings and/or tattoos are self-injurers trying to cope with emotions, while others with piercings and/or tattoos are simply expressing themselves.) Self-injury can also include a person who purposely puts him or herself in an unsafe situation with the goal of being injured. Examples of this include a person who participates in a violent sport or activity or instigates a conflict with someone else in the hope of getting hurt. Ultimately, a person who self-injures does so as a means of coping with overwhelming emotions.

Self-injury can be habit-forming, and it is just a temporary relief from emotional distress. When the emotions return, the person needs to self-injure again for relief. Self-injury can either numb a person to emotional pain, or it can create a feeling of euphoria to distract from the pain. When a child uses self-injury to escape distressing emotions, he or she does not learn healthy ways of coping with feelings. Consequently, self-injury becomes a frequently used method to cope with uncomfortable and/or painful emotions.

The most well known form of self-injury is cutting. Cutting is not a new behavior, but it is becoming more common. Children who cut will take any object that can penetrate skin, i.e.: razor, knife, pen cap, eraser and cut on their body until they get a mark or see blood. These children are often ashamed of their behavior. They hide their scars from others by wearing clothing to cover the marks, or they contend a cat, branches or an accident caused the cuts. Cutting is not limited to a gender, age group or ethnic group. Children from all backgrounds use cutting as a way to deal with intense emotions. Yet, like all forms of self-injury, cutting can lead to serious injury.

Children who use self-injury as a way to cope with feelings often cannot judge when they have gone too far. Children who cut can misjudge the depth of the cut and damage a major vein, or they can get an infection from the cuts. Children who use other forms of self-injury can cause permanent damage, as their judgment of what is safe is not accurate.

Children who use self-injury to cope with emotions need help. Their physical health is at risk, as they are purposely causing damage to their bodies. Additionally, they are in emotional pain, and they need to learn healthy ways of coping with their feelings. A mental health professional can teach children alternative ways of coping with emotions so they do not have to self-injure. Children can also be encouraged to talk to a trusted adult every time they feel the desire to self-injure. Other activities, which can release emotions in healthy ways include journaling, arts and crafts, and exercise. Parents who model healthy ways of handling their own emotions provide the most powerful lessons for children on how to cope with feelings. Parents who stay connected with their children can encourage their children to talk about problems rather than resorting to unhealthy behaviors to cope.

SUICIDE

Suicide is a problem with youth, and it is one of which parents need to be aware. When children become hopeless and feel they have no control over their lives, they might see suicide as the only way to feel better. Children who are feeling depressed are at a greater risk for committing suicide. Children who are considering suicide might give the following signs:

- isolating themselves from family and friends;
- a change in eating and/or sleeping habits;
- a change in mood and/or behavior;
- drug and alcohol abuse;
- neglecting personal appearance and hygiene;
- earning failing grades;
- showing a lack of interest in activities;
- asking questions or making statements such as, "What would you do if I disappeared?" or, "Nothing matters anymore. I won't be here much longer;"
- giving away belongings; and/or
- becoming suddenly happy after a period of depression.

Statements such as "I am going to kill myself," or "I wish I was dead," should always be taken seriously. If a child states that he or she is thinking about killing him or herself, regardless of the child's age, consultation with your child's health care provider, school counselor or another mental health professional should be considered for guidance regarding this issue. Even if the child is not serious about killing him or herself, the statement itself is a sign that the child needs to be noticed.

Children usually have a period of time where they experience stress and feel depressed before they consider suicide. When parents stay connected with their children, they will be more likely to detect if their children have a change in moods or behavior and know if there is a reason for concern. Childhood is such a tumultuous time, and children depend on their parents for emotional support as well as financial support. As a parent, you can model for your child healthy ways to cope with emotions so that your child will learn how to cope with intense feelings. Talk to your child daily about thoughts and feelings to help your child strengthen coping skills. When you are connected to your child, you will be able to monitor his or her emotional state, and you can guide your child through an emotionally healthy adolescence.

Consult with your school counselor, health care provider or the following websites for more information about stress, depression and suicide.

American Academy of Pediatrics, www.aap.org
American Academy of Child & Adolescent Psychiatry,
www.aacap.org
American Association of Suicidology, www.suicidology.org
American College of Obstetricians and Gynecologists,
www.acog.org
American Psychological Association, www.apa.org
American Self-Harm Information Clearinghouse,
www.selfinjury.org
National Mental Health Association, www.nmha.org
U.S. Department of Health and Human Services,
www.samhsa.gov
National Institute of Mental Health, www.nimh.nih.gov

21

Know the Signs of Alcohol and Drug Abuse

Tam's mom is concerned about his behavior. Tam is always tired and irritable. His grades are falling, and he has become very secretive about his activities. She knows that she cannot expect Tam to be the same loving little boy from a few years ago, but she did not expect for him to be so moody and unpredictable as a teenager. She wonders if he might be involved in drugs, but she does not want to cause more tension in their relationship by asking him. She is tempted to search his room, but she does not want to violate his privacy. Tam's mom decides to trust that the problem will resolve itself.

Alcohol and drug use, or substance abuse, among adolescents is becoming an epidemic. Drugs are readily available on high school and middle school campuses, and they are becoming a more common sight on elementary campuses. There is no longer an age that is "too young" to talk to children about drugs and alcohol. Media campaigns have warned parents and teenagers for years about the dangers of drug and alcohol use, but the problem is getting worse. Children are dying every day from drug overdoses, alcohol poisoning, and drug and alcohol related car accidents. Drugs and alcohol are usually available

145

at teenage parties--even if adults are present. Some adults allow their children to drink or use drugs as long as they do it at home in the presence of the parent. Adolescents, though, do not have the physical or emotional maturity to set limits for substance abuse. The part of the brain responsible for impulse control does not fully develop until the early 20's. (For more information about adolescent brain development, log on to www.nimh.nih.gov/publicat/teenbrain.cfm) For this reason, adolescents display riskier behavior. They are more likely to make dangerous choices, and many adolescents lack the ability to know how to set safe limits when consuming substances. Drugs and alcohol can damage this developing part of the brain that controls impulse control, and substances can affect its healthy development. Additionally, the physical and emotional immaturity of adolescents put them at a higher risk than adults for becoming addicted to substances. This one issue is having a major impact on our society. Minds are being permanently damaged from alcohol and drug use; minds that have the potential for greatness. Financial resources are being drained in an effort to combat drug and alcohol addictions. Countless crimes are committed by people under the influence who have impaired judgment or who are looking for money to continue their addictive habits. Children of all ages have to be educated about the effects of drug and alcohol use because it can be found everywhere, and its impact is far reaching. Parents are on the frontline of educating their children. Children need to know the facts, and they need to ultimately learn to ask themselves, "How is choosing to use this substance going to affect me now and in the future?"

Children who are involved in drugs and alcohol will have a greater challenge with being successful in school. The use of a mind-altering substance affects brain development, attention, behavior and motivation. These children no longer care about school or their future; they only think about the next time they are going to use alcohol or drugs. Substance abuse can also lead to illegal activities, as children need to find ways of getting money to purchase the alcohol and drugs. Children may begin by experimenting with drugs or alcohol, but the initial sensation they get when they first try a drug or drink alcohol will quickly diminish. They begin to need more and more of the substance to obtain the same level of feeling high. This begins the cycle of addiction. Children do not have the same physical capacity as adults to withstand the effects of alcohol or drug use. Their bodies continue to grow and develop into adulthood. They are more susceptible than adults to becoming addicted to substances, and their bodies have a more intense reaction to the chemicals. There is no safe way for children to use drugs or alcohol. They can die from a first time use. Parents are the most effective deterrent to drug and alcohol abuse. All parents should have a zero tolerance stance when it comes to drug and alcohol use among their children. One drink, one smoke or one pill is one too many. The best way to prevent children from abusing substances is to educate them about the effects of using drugs and alcohol.

TOBACCO

Koto: I want to play football.

Counselor: That's great. When are tryouts?

Koto: It doesn't matter because I can't play.

Counselor: Why not?

Koto: I have been smoking for a while, and I can't run very far without losing my breath. But, I would have loved to play.

According to the 2003 Youth Risk Behavior Surveillance report from the Department of Health and Human Services, more than 20 percent of high school students reported that they smoked a cigarette before the age of 13. Children in elementary school need to be taught about the dangers of smoking or chewing tobacco, and this should be a discussion that continues throughout adolescence. Children who start smoking or chewing tobacco at a young age are more likely to become addicted. Adolescent bodies are still developing, and they are more susceptible to the affects of nicotine. Children who smoke are more prone to getting sick which causes them to miss school, and they are more likely to have a diminished lung capacity. The long-term effects of smoking are well-known including an increased likelihood of developing lung cancer, emphysema and heart disease.

Parents are the primary educators for children about the effects of smoking. Talk to your child about the dangers of smoking. Look for opportunities to broach the topic including seeing someone else smoking when you are in public or discussing an advertisement promoting smoking. Be sure your child clearly understands that smoking is not acceptable. Talk about the short-term consequences such as bad breath, yellow teeth, and limited lung capacity. Discuss how much peer pressure your child feels in regards to smoking, and talk about how to handle the pressure. Remind your child that the majority of adolescents do not smoke, and there are healthier ways to spend time and money. If your child is already smoking and cannot stop, he or she might be addicted. Consult with your health care provider about recommended programs or treatments to stop smoking. If you smoke, seriously consider stopping for your health as well as the health of your child. Educate your child about living a healthy lifestyle through your words and actions.

ALCOHOL

Marcia cannot believe she is in prison. She wakes up every morning and cries when she realizes where she is. This is not how her life was supposed to be like. She should be a freshman in college right now like all of her friends. She had a scholarship to go to school, and she was going to major in advertising. She is still in shock that it is all gone. Ten months ago, she decided to drive home after drinking at a party. She never made it. She crashed into another car in an oncoming lane, and two people were killed. They never made it home, and neither did she. She went from the crash scene to the jail cell to prison. Two people are now dead, and their families are devastated. Her parents are heartbroken. She never made it home.

Many children and parents are not concerned with adolescent drinking. They do not consider the health and safety risks from drinking as serious. I often have children tell me that they drink at family get-togethers, and their parents are giving them the drinks. Children should not be allowed to drink alcohol at any time. Children can become addicted to alcohol, and their behavior, while under the influence of alcohol, can lead to illegal activities and health risks—including death. Parents are the best deterrents to preventing their children from using alcohol.

Children need to be taught at an early age about the dangers of drinking, and this conversation should continue throughout adolescence. You need to be very clear with your child about your values and attitudes regarding alcohol. Discussions about alcohol with young children can occur whenever the opportunity presents itself through television commercials or seeing a relative who is drunk. Children this age can be taught about the negative affects of alcohol on the body, and they can learn what it means to live a healthy lifestyle. As children get older, they can learn more specific facts about the short and long-term affects of alcohol, what the consequences are if alcohol is abused, and how alcohol affects a developing body. Children's friends should be included in these discussions so that they can be a support group for each other to resist drinking. Alcohol facts include the following information.

- Alcohol has a greater effect on children and adolescents, and it can damage every organ in a child's body.
- Alcohol inhibits self-control leading to risky behaviors such as vandalism, violence and sexual activity.
- Using alcohol while on medication is very risky and can lead to death.
- Drinking large amounts of alcohol in a short time period may cause alcohol poisoning.
- Alcohol can cause weight gain and bad breath.

For more facts on alcohol abuse, visit www.samhsa.gov.

Your child should be well educated about alcohol facts by the time he or she is a teenager. You need to stay committed to maintaining an open and healthy relationship with your child during this time so that he or she can come to you if help is needed with resisting alcohol.

Teenagers might act like they do not want parents involved with their lives, but they need parental guidance during this time just as much as when they were younger.

The following suggestions will help your child to develop the skills needed to resist alcohol use.

- Give your child questions to ask when offered a drink such as, "What is the drink?" "Where did it come from?" "What is in it?" Your child should know never to drink something that is not safe.
- Help your child come up with reasons as to why he or she is not interested in drinking. These could include, "It makes me sick." "I have to get up early in the morning." "I have to go to work later."
- Remind your child that he or she should always leave a situation that is uncomfortable. Tell your child that you can always be called to pick him or her up regardless of the time or location.
- Talk to your child about the dangers of riding in the car with someone who has been drinking. Look with your child at the websites for Mothers Against Drunk Driving, www.madd.org, and Students Against Destructive Decisions www.saddonline. org for more information about the tragedy of drunk driving.

Children need to practice resisting peer pressure for all situations. Role-play different scenarios involving alcohol with your child so he or she can practice saying "No" and strengthen his or her resistance skills for those situations. Be clear and specific with your child when discussing your opinion about using alcohol. Your child needs to understand that you do not approve of substance use for him or her, his or her friends or yourself.

You will probably be asked by your child "If you can drink, why can't I?" Be prepared for this question. Teach your child that young bodies are still developing, and alcohol has a greater effect on young bodies. Adult bodies are more resistant to the effects of alcohol than younger bodies. Be aware of how much you drink in the presence of your child. If your child is developing a drinking problem, you might want to consider throwing out all of the liquor in your home and not drinking around your child. If you have liquor hidden in your home, your child probably knows where it is, and he or she might be drinking the liquor. Be aware of what is available to your child and pay attention to your own behavior. Your healthy lifestyle is the best role model for your child.

Children who abuse alcohol often do not quit without help—they need someone else to intervene. The following symptoms can indicate that a child is abusing alcohol:

- an abrupt change in mood, attitude, personality and behavior;
- a sudden decline in school attendance, and/or lack of interest in school performance;
- a decline in grades;
- a lack of ambition;
- a resistance to discipline at home or at school;
- difficult relationships with family and friends;
- withdrawing from family and friends;
- a change in appetite, sleep habits and/or hygiene;
- dishonesty and secretiveness;
- exhibiting violent behavior, showing sudden outbreak of temper, and/or overreacting to criticism;
- frequently borrowing money from family and friends and/or stealing;
- having slurred speech and/or confused thinking; and/or
- using poor judgment and showing a loss of short-term memory (U.S. Department of Health and Human Services, *Tips for Teens*).

These signs can be symptoms of alcohol abuse or another problem. Consult with a professional if your child is exhibiting these symptoms. There are screening tests available to use with children for detecting alcohol use. Talk with your health care provider or pharmacist about what products are available. Children who come from families that have a history of substance abuse are at a higher risk for developing an abuse problem. These children need to learn the facts about the dangers of alcohol abuse at an early age, and they should be monitored closely for signs of abuse.

The best method for helping your child resist alcohol is to stay connected with your child. Talk to your child daily about school and friends. Maintain an open communication with your child, and be the safe person to whom your child can turn if there is a problem. Stay involved in your child's life by knowing his or her friends and activities. Praise your child often, and help him or her find ways of being successful. Keep your child's life active, structured and enjoyable. Staying connected with your child and educating your child about alcohol facts are the best methods for preventing alcohol abuse.

DRUGS

> *Counselor: When did you start using drugs?*
>
> *Abel: When I was three.*
>
> *Counselor: How did you start using drugs when you were three years old?*
>
> *Abel: My grandmother gave me a joint to smoke.*

Drugs are everywhere. Drugs have touched every school in which I have worked. Children in elementary schools are even exposed to drugs. It is an epidemic. Drug prevention, like alcohol prevention, requires parental involvement. Parents need to be aware of the most common drugs available to students; how to prevent their children from choosing to use drugs; and how to detect drug use in their children. This can feel like an ominous task, but parents who learn the basics about drug abuse can have a profound impact on their children's health and safety.

The challenge of drug awareness is learning what drugs might be available for children. The following is a brief explanation of drugs children typically abuse. More information about these and other drugs can be found on the websites listed at the end of this chapter.

- Marijuana—This is one of the most well known drugs abused by children. Marijuana is a plant that is smoked usually in rolled up paper, a hollowed-out cigar (known as a blunt), a pipe or a bong. The active ingredient, THC, affects the nerve cells in the part of the brain where memories are formed. Marijuana use can alter mood and coordination, elevate the heart rate or blood pressure, and damage lungs. Many of today's parents smoked marijuana in their youth, so they are not concerned when they learn their children are using marijuana. The marijuana that is available today, though, is more toxic. It can be mixed with other unknown substances making it more dangerous to inhale. Marijuana is known as a gateway drug meaning that once children try marijuana, they are more likely to try other drugs.

- Inhalants—Inhalants are so dangerous because they are easy to obtain, and someone can die the first time they are used which is known as Sudden Sniffing Death Syndrome. Inhalants are gas or vapors that are intentionally sniffed or huffed to create an immediate high. Inhalants can by ingested by breathing the chemicals directly from the container, spraying the chemical into a paper bag and inhaling, or soaking a rag in the chemical and holding the rag in the mouth. There are hundreds of products that can be used as inhalants including spray paint, paint thinner, glue, gasoline, propane, nail polish remover, air freshener, correction fluid, marker pen, air-conditioning refrigerant, products that contain air in a can used to clean electronic equipment, and cleaning fluid. Inhalant use immediately affects the brain with great speed and force, and it can cause seizures, permanent physical damage or sudden death. Chronic use can lead to permanent damage of daily functions such as walking and talking. Children need to know how to use products such as finger nail polish remover or paint thinner in a safe way to prevent inhaling the chemicals.

- Methamphetamine--This drug is known as speed, crank, meth and various other street names. Methamphetamine is highly addictive, and it is becoming one of the most abused drugs by both adolescents and adults. This drug can be taken orally, smoked, injected or snorted. Methamphetamine gives a person a false sense of energy where he or she will go days without sleeping. This drug affects the brain by causing mood swings, depression and anxiety. Users will no longer care about how they look, their grades, their jobs, their relationships or their futures. Their only concern is getting the next high. Long-term effects include weight-loss, hair loss, paranoia, liver and kidney damage and heart problems.

- Over-the-Counter Drugs—Over-the-counter medication creates difficulties for parents because they serve a legitimate purpose in treating symptoms related to illnesses. Children who want to alter their moods, though, can abuse these drugs. Some cough and cold medicines contain an ingredient called dextromethorphan (DXM) that can act as a hallucinogen when taken in high doses. When these drugs are consumed in high doses, children can experience a variety of dangerous physical effects including confusion, paranoia, irregular heartbeat, high blood pressure, loss of motor control and brain damage. These drugs can be purchased by anyone at the local drug store, yet they can lead to addiction and physical damage when abused.

- Steroids—Steroids are often illegally used to help improve athletic performance. They are only safe and legal to use when prescribed and monitored by a physician. Steroids can be addictive, and they can affect appearance, mood, and physical health.

- Prescription Drugs—Prescription drug abuse is a growing problem among adolescents. Prescription drugs, like steroids, can easily be obtained by opening the home medicine cabinet or ordering them off of the Internet. These drugs are used to treat anxiety, depression, sleep disorders, ADHD, to relieve pain, and numerous other conditions. Adolescents can abuse these drugs to alter their mood, energy and perception. Many people do not perceive these drugs as dangerous because they are legally prescribed for diagnosed conditions. Consequently, adolescents are not cautious when taking these drugs or sharing them with friends.

- Hallucinogens—These drugs come in various forms including LSD, Ecstasy, and PCP. They affect perception, reality, time and senses. Users often report hearing voices and seeing images that do not exist. Hallucinogens can cause physical and emotional problems including panic attacks. The intense effects of the drug can last for hours. The tolerance level for hallucinogens rises quickly, so more and more of the drug is needed to achieve the same effect. People have reported having hallucinogen-induced flashbacks years after they have stopped using the drug. LSD can be licked or sucked off of small squares of paper that might be decorated with cartoon characters or colorful designs. Hallucinogens can also be snorted or swallowed in capsules or liquid forms. Marigold seeds and other plant seeds are becoming popular hallucinogens. The seeds are brewed in a coffee pot, and the liquid is swallowed to create a drug-induced effect.

• Club Drugs—This term refers to drugs that are generally available at raves (all-night dance parties), nightclubs and concerts. There are a variety of different club drugs including Ecstasy, GHB, and Rohypnol. Ecstasy comes in a powder, tablet or capsule form that can be swallowed or snorted. GHB (gamma hydroxybutyrate) is usually in a liquid form that is colorless and tasteless and can be mistaken for water. Rohypnol comes as a pill which is swallowed. Club drugs affect the brain by affecting senses, judgment and memory, and they can cause hallucinations. These drugs also have physical affects including nausea, sweating, chills, breathing problems and seizures. These drugs are dangerous because they can be put into someone's drink, and the person would not be aware of it. Consequently, a person can have a serious physical reaction or pass-out and become the victim of an assault. These drugs are also likely to be taken while drinking which creates a dangerous combination of drugs and alcohol. Caution your child to never leave a drink unattended at a party, avoid drinking the homemade party punch, and never allow someone else to bring him or her a drink.

• Cocaine—Cocaine can come in a powder form or a rock form called crack. Cocaine can be snorted through the nose or injected with a needle, and crack is smoked. Crack and cocaine cause a short and intense high immediately followed by depressed feelings and cravings for more of the drug. It is highly addictive as more and more of the drug is needed to feel "normal." Users can die the first time they try the drug. Crack and cocaine are expensive, and users can spend up to thousands of dollars a week for the drug.

- Heroin—This is one of the most highly addictive drugs because it enters the brain quickly and affects the parts of the brain responsible for producing physical dependence. Heroin can be injected, smoked or snorted, and it comes in a white to dark brown powder substance to a tar-like substance. Heroine can lead to many health problems. Overdosing with heroin is easy because its effects are often unpredictable (U.S. Department of Health and Human Services, *Tips for Teens*).

Children who are abusing drugs exhibit many signs indicating that they are using drugs. These symptoms mirror the symptoms seen in children who abuse alcohol. They include:

- an abrupt change in mood, attitude, personality and behavior;
- a sudden decline in school attendance and/or lack of interest in school performance;
- a decline in grades;
- a lack of ambition;
- a resistance to discipline at home or at school;
- increasingly difficult relationships with family and friends;
- a withdrawal from family and friends;
- a change in friends;
- a change in appetite, sleep habits and/or hygiene;
- dishonesty or secretiveness;
- exhibiting violent behavior, sudden outbreak of temper, and/or overreacting to criticism;
- frequently borrowing money from family and friends and/or stealing;
- a slurring of speech and/or confused thinking;
- using poor judgment and having loss of short-term memory;
- unexplained empty cold and cough remedy packages in the trash can; and/or

• unexplained empty aerosol cans in the trash.

Consult with a professional if your child exhibits any of these signs. They might mean that your child is becoming involved in drugs, or they might be signs of another problem. A qualified professional can help you determine what is causing the changes in your child's behavior.

Children need help the first time they try drugs. Intervening with children in the early stages of drug use is far more effective than waiting until children become regular users. Children's bodies are still developing, so they do not have the tolerance for resisting the effects of addiction. Children will become addicted to drugs quicker than adults simply because of their immature bodies. When parents intervene early and give consequences for their children's drug use, the children are more likely to stop using the drugs because they do not want to experience the consequences. When children are more heavily involved in drugs, they care more about experiencing their addictive high than suffering a consequence. It is more difficult to help children at this stage. Drug screening products can be used to help determine if a child is using drugs, and a health care provider or pharmacist can guide parents in learning about available drug screening products. Often times, children in the early stages of drug use will stop if they know that they will be randomly screened. The fear of the consequence for getting caught is stronger than the desire for the drug. Additionally, telling children that their homes will be searched by law enforcement if drug use is suspected is another deterrent to drug use. Local law enforcement agencies can be consulted with to learn about this process and the consequences of finding drugs in the home. Regardless of the level of involvement a child has in drug use, consultation with school counselors or another professional is recommended. A child who is using drugs will benefit from intervention to learn how to make healthier choices and avoid the dangerous practice of substance abuse.

Children who are abusing any addictive substance are putting themselves at risk for physical, emotional and mental problems. Children who abuse substances are less likely to be successful in school.

The lure of addictive substances is very strong. Children are often unprepared to resist the temptation these substances offer. The best defense children have against resisting the temptation to try a drug is to be educated about the facts of substance abuse and to have a healthy relationship with their parents.

Begin talking to your child at an early age about the dangers of substance abuse. Continue this conversation throughout adolescence. Be wary of lecturing your child about substance abuse because he or she is not likely to listen. Instead, talk to your child about what you know and ask your child what he or she knows. Ask open-ended questions such as, "What do you know about drinking and driving," or "Tell me what you know about cigarettes." Ask your child to tell you about people he or she knows who abuse substances and discuss what this person's life might be like. Share stories that you know regarding substance abuse, and give your child the facts. If you are connected to your child, your child will be more likely to come to you regarding issues related to tobacco, drugs and alcohol, and you will be more apt to notice the signs if your child starts abusing substances. Your child's health and future depend on you being proactive in the area of substance abuse. The only way to ensure that a child does not become addicted to drugs is for the child to not try a drug—even one time. No one knows why some people become addicted to substances and others do not, but it is not worth the risk to find out to which category your child belongs. Be the best teacher for your child by refraining from smoking or consuming substances—at least in your child's presence. Help your child have the best chance for success in school and life by teaching him or her the importance of remaining drug free. Consult with your school counselor or the following websites for more information about substance abuse.

American Academy of Child and Adolescent Psychiatry, www.aacap.org
American Academy of Pediatrics, www.aap.org
Free Vibe, www.freevibe.com
Kids Health, www.kidshealth.org

National Center for Chronic Disease Prevention and Health Promotion, www.cdc.gov/tobacco

National Clearinghouse for Alcohol and Drug Information, www.health.org

National Inhalant Prevention Coalition, www.inhalants.org

National Institute on Drug Abuse, www.nida.nih.gov

National Institute on Alcohol Abuse and Alcoholism, www.niaaa.nih.gov

Partnership for a Drug Free America, www.drugfreeamerica.org

Substance Abuse and Mental Health Administration, www.samhsa.gov

The Choking Game: Although the choking game does not fall under the category of substance abuse, children engage in this activity to obtain a "high" feeling, so it is included at the end of this chapter. The choking game, as it is commonly referred, involves shutting off oxygen to the brain by choking, strangling, or putting pressure on the chest. When the child regains consciousness, he or she experiences an intense rush similar to a high experienced by drug use. Children believe this activity is safe because they are not ingesting substances. This activity is popular among young adolescents who want to experience a high without using drugs. These children do not realize that they can die from this game. This activity is popular at parties, but more children are engaging in it alone in their bedrooms. This activity can be addictive. There are numerous Internet sites dedicated to promoting the choking game which adds to its danger. Talk to your child about this activity and its dangers. Be sure your child understands that obstructing the flow of oxygen to the brain can lead to brain damage and death. If your child continues to engage in this activity and you have concerns about your child's health, consult with a health care provider for guidance.

22

Be Aware of the Signs of Gang Involvement

Counselor: Ms. Green, I came to see you because I am concerned about your son. I have been talking to Roland for several weeks, and today he admitted to me that he is involved in a gang. He told me he wants help.

Ms. Green: You know, the school's been telling me this for years, but it is just not possible. Roland is a good boy. When I asked him if he is in a gang, he tells me, "No."

Counselor: A child will often not admit to his parents that he is in a gang. He might not want to disappoint his parents, or he might be afraid of the consequences. But, Roland told me today that he is in a gang, and he wants to get out. Yet, he does not believe it is possible.

Ms. Green: I just don't believe it. I don't let him go anywhere, so I don't see how he is in a gang. If my son were in a gang, he would tell me.

Counselor: Ms. Green, perhaps you can come to the school and meet with Roland and me so that we can discuss this together.

We often do not want to hear the truth--especially about our own children. I was telling this mother point blank that her son had admitted that he was in a gang, and he was asking for help to leave the gang life. Yet, she still could not accept this truth about her baby. When I have to meet with parents to discuss their children's involvement in a gang, I am usually met with denials. Parents often do not want to face the reality that their children have detoured down a dangerous and forbidden path. Yet, the denial that allows parents to ignore the truths about their children is the same denial that gives their children the freedom to make dangerous choices in the first place. These choices affect how well students perform in school and their overall well-being. Students who are involved in gangs will have a more difficult time achieving success in school. Gang involvement often leads to discipline problems in school and failing grades. Students who are involved in gangs are less likely to set high goals for themselves regarding education and careers. The focus of children in gangs is to do whatever needs to be done to keep the gang strong and feared. Their energy is directed towards the gang rather than school. Gangs are usually involved in some type of drug activity and other illegal activities. The combination of drugs and violence is deadly. Adults who have been in the gang life for years often are the gang leaders. These adults influence young adolescents to participate in violent or illegal activities for the good of the gang. For many children, once they become associated with a gang, their lives are in constant danger as well as the lives of their family members. Involvement in a gang can lead to prison or death. If an adolescent decides he or she wants to get out of gang, that decision can often be just as dangerous as remaining in the gang. Gang leaders do not like their members to leave, so they use threats and violence to keep their members. Parents need to be aware of the problems of gangs for the safety of their children.

Many people believe that gang activity occurs somewhere else—not in their neighborhood. Yet, according to the Centers for Disease Control and Prevention 2002 National Youth Gang Survey, there are more than 24,500 different youth gangs around the country, and more than 772,500 teens and young adults involved in gangs. If you see graffiti in your neighborhood, then there is a good chance that a gang is operating nearby and they can influence your children. Children join gangs for attention and to make friends; for the excitement of being involved in something forbidden; because of peer pressure; and/or for protection in school or the neighborhood. Gangs affect children, and they have a profound impact on children's success in school as well as their overall health. It is much easier to prevent children from joining a gang than it is to try to get them out of a gang. There are a variety of ways that you can discourage your child from becoming involved in a gang.

- Spend time with your child and get to know his or her friends. Trust your instinct when you meet your child's friends, and closely monitor your child's relationship with another child who makes you uncomfortable.

- Your child needs to be involved with activities. Children who do not have friends or who have a lot of free time are prime candidates for gang involvement.

- Nurture your relationship with your child so that you will notice if he or she does begin to behave differently. When you discuss gangs with your child, teach him or her to think, "How will joining a gang affect me now and in the future?" This is more effective than simply telling your child he or she is not allowed to join a gang.

- Learn what gang-style clothing is in your neighborhood, and do not allow your child to dress in this style. Even if your child is not in a gang, this type of dress will attract the attention of gangs. Gang descriptors can be as simple as shoestring color or what side of the forehead the bill of a cap is leaning.

- Set a reasonable curfew for your child, and do not allow him or her to stay out past the curfew time. Do not allow your child to go to places where there is no adult supervision.

- Learn what gang writing and gang symbols look like, and do not allow your child to write like this on papers, books, clothing or any place else. Teach your child to respect property.

- Talk to your child about gangs and learn from your child what kind of activity might be occurring in your neighborhood.

- Become informed about gang activity in your neighborhood. Attend community meetings; read related articles; talk to your school administrators and school police; and get information from your local police or sheriff's department.
- Be involved in your neighborhood. Know your neighbors, and discourage gangs from hanging around your neighborhood. Paint over graffiti in your neighborhood as soon as it appears.

Children who are involved in gang activities live their lives in secret. They hide the truth from their parents because they know their choices are unacceptable. Yet, they are still kids, and they need their parents to know the truth before it is too late. Parents are the most powerful influence in keeping their children safe. If you are concerned that your child might be involved in a gang, talk to him or her about your concerns. Be honest with your child about why you are concerned that he or she might be involved in a gang. Talk to your school administrators and school police. Get as much information as you can from other people about how your child behaves at school and who his or her friends are. School officials are good resources for learning about your child's activities. If you learn your child is in a gang, talk to your police or sheriff's department. Ask them for guidance about what steps you should take to get your child out of the gang. It might be as simple as your child not hanging around the gang anymore, or you might have to move to a different neighborhood. Lastly, seek counseling for your child. This will help your child discover the reasons why he or she chose to join a gang, and it will help your child learn different ways to get his or her needs met. Involvement in gangs not only affects school success, but it can drastically change your child's future. Your child needs you to be actively involved in his or her life so that success in the future can be a reality.

23

Talk to Your Child about Intimacy and Sex

Amelia wonders if she is pregnant. She has only had sex one time with her boyfriend, and he told her that she could not get pregnant if it was the first time. They did not use a condom, but Amelia is still worried about being pregnant.

The youngest pregnant student that I have had was eleven years old. I usually have several students each year who are pregnant which means that there are many more students having sex who have had abortions or have not become pregnant. Children are having sex. Children from all ages (including elementary school), ethnic groups and economic backgrounds are having sex. Children who are sexually active are risking the potential of their futures. Pregnancy, disease and emotional difficulties, which often result from premarital sex, can all affect success. It is no longer an option to wait until children start puberty to talk about sex. The discussion needs to begin years earlier, and parents need to initiate the discussion.

SEXUALITY DISCUSSION

Raimi: Mom, what are those people doing?

Mom: They're kissing because they love each other.

Raimi: You say you love me but you don't kiss me like that.

Mom: There are different kinds of way to show love. That is a special way that two adults show they love each other. We show we love each other with kisses on our cheeks and hugs.

Raimi: I like our way better.

Mom: Yeah, me too.

Discussions about sexuality and intimacy often occur at unexpected moments. Parents are given many opportunities to discuss different aspects of sex and relationships. Many parents rely on schools to teach their children about the biology of conception. Yet, sexuality encompasses far more than the physical act. Children need to learn about the emotional component of having sex and the risks and responsibilities that are inherent with being sexually active. This type of discussion is limited in a school setting. The responsibility falls to parents to talk to their children about sex, intimacy and relationships. The messages that children receive about sex from the media, the Internet and peers are often inaccurate and confusing. Without a clear understanding of sexuality and all of its complexities, children are more likely to make unhealthy choices. Children need parents to provide them structure and guidance in the area of sexuality, and they need to know that their parents are safe people to turn to for factual information about sex.

You set the tone for your discussions with your child about this issue. Even if your child appears uncomfortable, you model that discussions about sexuality between a parent and a child are healthy and necessary. Your child will learn to be comfortable with the discussions if you are comfortable with them. There are many books available to help parents talk to their children about this issue. Visit your local bookstore or library to find out what age-appropriate books are available on this issue. You can also get advice on how to approach this discussion from your school counselor, minister or health care provider.

It is natural for children to turn to parents for advice and guidance in the area of sex and relationships because they understand that their parents have experience in these areas. You will not have just one discussion about sex and intimacy with your child. These discussions will begin at an early age when toddlers begin to notice physical differences in gender, and they will continue long into your child's adulthood. Young children will question from where babies come. As children age and their curiosity grows, the questions will expand to include deeper discussions about how a child is conceived. Children in later elementary grades may question more about what it means to have a boyfriend or a girlfriend and wonder about kissing. Middle school children are more exposed to sex in peer conversations, the media and Internet. The discussion for this age can begin to include what it means to be responsible with sexuality, what the consequences are for having sex, and how to make healthy choices. High school students need to be educated about the specific consequences of being sexually active including unplanned pregnancies and sexually transmitted diseases. Many high school students—and some middle school students--are of the age when they are considering having sex, so discussions of intimacy and emotions related to having sex with someone are essential. Children will also have questions about masturbation, menstruation, oral sex, and contraception. Be prepared to answer these questions so you can maintain a comfortable and open communication with your child. Additionally, include in your discussions with your older child what "consent" means. Be sure your child understands the ramifications that can result for anyone who engages in sexual activity--including oral sex and fondling--with someone who does not give consent or who is not legally old enough to give consent. Discuss the consequences that can occur for the perpetrator as well as the victim when consent is not given and a sexual assault occurs.

Allow your child to set the pace for your discussions on sex and intimacy. Children of the same age have different levels of maturity, so allow your child to determine what the topics will be for your discussions. Also, be prepared for questions your child might have when he or she is exposed to an advertisement or public exhibition regarding sex. Ultimately, communicate with your child that every question is important, and your child should feel comfortable talking to you about sexuality and relationships.

Children need to have a clear understanding of your values and expectations regarding sex. They will use your guidelines as a guide for their behavior. Be clear with your child if your family values oppose premarital sex, but allow your child the freedom to talk to you if they are considering engaging in sex anyway.

CONSEQUENCES

Lan knows something is wrong. He knows every time he urinates, but he doesn't want to think about it—he doesn't want to deal with it. So, he just ignores it and hopes it will go away.

Your discussions about the consequences of engaging in premarital sex should be a part of every conversation with your adolescent. Emphasize to your older child that having sex, including oral sex, can create countless problems. Have an open discussion with your child about how easy it is to become pregnant and how an unplanned pregnancy can drastically alter his or her future. The National Campaign to Prevent Teen Pregnancy website at www.teenpregnancy.org can assist you in this discussion. It is also essential that you discuss sexually transmitted diseases (STDs) with you child so that he or she will have factual information. Children often do not consider the consequence of getting an STD when having sex, so they are a high-risk group for contracting diseases. Your health care provider, school counselor, or public health office should have pamphlets to guide you in your discussion about STDs. Additional information about talking to your children about STDs can be found on www.kidshealth.org and www.familydoctor.org.

SEXUAL ABUSE

Kathy doesn't understand what is the matter with her. She has had many boyfriends, and she always does what they want. She believes that if she does whatever her boyfriend wants he will always love her. But, her boyfriends always end up leaving her, and she feels used.

Children who are sexually active with multiple partners or children who attempt to be sexual in their dress and behavior could be exhibiting signs that they were victims of sexual abuse, or they might be coping with another issue. If a child acts out sexually, consultation with a health care provider or school counselor is recommended. The child might need to go to counseling to gain an understanding as to why he or she is behaving in a sexual way and to learn healthier ways of coping with emotions.

SEXUAL IDENTITY

Yvette is terrified. She is finding herself attracted to girls, and she does not know what to do. All of her friends talk about how cute boys are, but she doesn't feel the same way. She does not know who to talk to. Her parents will disown her, and her friends will think she is a freak. She is panicked that someone will figure out her secret.

Many children question their sexual identity. There are children who feel they are gay or lesbian, and these children need someone to talk to about their feelings. If your child believes that he or she is gay or lesbian, you cannot ignore this fact or forbid them to not feel a certain way. If you do not feel comfortable talking to your child about his or her feelings, find someone else to whom your child can talk. Children who identify as gay or lesbian struggle with feeling different, and they are at-risk for engaging in unhealthy behaviors as a way to cope with their feelings. Children who wonder if they are gay or lesbian can come to a better understanding of their feelings if they have a safe and nurturing person to ask questions and share emotions. A school counselor can provide resources for further information about gay and lesbian adolescents. Parents and Friends and Families of Lesbians and Gays, www.pflag.org, is an excellent site for parents struggling with this issue.

Adolescents struggle with sexuality issues. There are too many teenage pregnancies resulting in students dropping out of school. Other students contract STDs, and they are shocked to learn that because of the disease, they may not be able to have children later. Many girls and boys believe everything their current love interest tells them, and they, thus, have sex and are devastated later to find out they had been used. Students have questions, and they often look for answers in the media, the Internet or among friends. Children who are struggling with issues related to sexuality and relationships often let their academic grades decline because they cannot concentrate on schoolwork. Children need guidance with sexuality and intimacy. Children need their parents to provide the guidance and safety required to learn about sexuality and relationships, and this communication needs to begin at a young age. Sex is a confusing topic for all ages, and parents can help their children learn how to be responsible and make healthy choices so they can successfully maneuver through this confusing time of growth and development. Children who learn how to make healthy choices and treat their bodies with respect will grow into adults who find success and happiness in relationships.

24

Define Your Values and Spiritual Beliefs

Counselor: Ralph, where do you see yourself in ten years?

Ralph: I don't know.

Counselor: Well, what goals have you set for yourself?

Ralph: None.

*Counselor: What do you see yourself doing with your life?
What matters to you? What gets you excited?*

Ralph: Nothing.

Counselor: Do you believe you have a purpose for being here?

Ralph: No.

Ralph was sixteen years old when we had this conversation, and it is not an uncommon conversation. Many children have not been taught to look into the future and make plans. These children do not understand that their life has a purpose, and what they value guides their life in this purpose. If a child feels that he or she has no purpose, then that child is at-risk for depression, failure and engaging in unhealthy behaviors. Children must be taught that they matter. They must have a set of values by which to live. Children need to be taught values that will help them make healthy and positive choices and ultimately find their purpose in the world. Children need to believe that their presence in this world does make a difference.

Children learn how to move in the world based on the teachings of their parents. They learn what is important and what values are worth fighting for from their parents. When parents do not take the time to teach and model values and purpose for their children, children have no direction. Children are not born with a ready character and focus. They are sponges waiting for their parents to teach them about values, life and purpose. I can instantly spot the children who feel they have no purpose. They slump a little more than their peers. They look down more often. They mumble their words and are sluggish in their world. They do not see a reason for getting up each morning, and they struggle to make it through the school day. They do not see a reason for learning in school or for developing healthy relationships. When bad things happen, they just shrug them off with the attitude of, "That is just what life is like." They are not able to see the bigger picture beyond the present moment of their life. The teachings of parents will give children direction and provide children with a greater understanding of their purpose in the world.

VALUES

Mary: Dad, why do we have to spend our Saturdays at the soup kitchen? All of my other friends get to sleep late, but I have to come here.

Dad: Mary, we are very fortunate to have a place to sleep and food to eat. We have a responsibility to help others who are struggling to make it.

Mary: I know. I just don't want to have to spend my Saturdays here.

Dad: Well, our family believes in helping others. If you really don't like coming on Saturday, we can find something else for you to do.

Mary: Thanks Dad. I want to help others, but maybe I can do something during the week.

Purpose gives children direction, and values provide them with a structure. Children must be taught right and wrong by their parents and be given a blueprint of values on which they depend for making choices. Every family will differ in their beliefs of what is right and wrong, but children need some structure for making sense of their world. This structure comes from the family. Children will adopt the values and beliefs of their parents until they are able to think abstractly and start questioning the beliefs of the parents. Children will eventually question the values and lessons that their parents have taught them, but this is normal. Children are discovering their individuality when they question their parents' teaching. They are in the process of creating their own values by which to live. Children will take ownership of their beliefs by defining their own values by which to guide their lives. These might be the same values and beliefs of their parents or they might be different, but it will likely be a combination of both. Children who have a clear understanding of their family's values will have the structure and security needed for making healthy and good choices as their identity develops.

SPIRITUALITY

Emma: Do you believe in God?

Liz: I don't know.

Emma: Well, what does your family believe?

Liz: I don't know. We never talk about it.

Emma: Do you go to church?

Liz: I went once when my Uncle Clay died. It was kind of weird.

Emma: Why was it weird?

Liz: I had just been talking to Uncle Clay the day before he died, and then the next time I saw him it was in a church and he was in a coffin. I didn't like it.

Emma: Where do you think your uncle is now?

Liz: I don't know. It doesn't really matter. He's not here anymore.

Spirituality provides an anchor from which many families form their values, and spirituality helps people define their purpose. Families who neglect incorporating spirituality into their lifestyle create a challenge for children. Children need to have an understanding of why families believe as they do and why the world functions as it does. Spiritual beliefs provide these answers for children. I often have children who have been told about what is right and wrong, but they do not understand what makes an action right or wrong or why it matters. These children do not have the benefit of seeing the whole picture of why it is important to make healthy and positive choices. Ultimately, their commitment to follow their family's teachings is weak, and they are easily influenced to make unhealthy choices. Providing a spiritual foundation for children will help them make sense of the world when they encounter experiences that challenge their knowledge of how the world is supposed to work.

The traditional way of incorporating spirituality into a family is attending church and becoming involved in church activities. Yet, a family can also experience spirituality in other ways.

- Appreciate nature and the larger world through camping trips or walks in the park.
- Spend quiet time meditating and then share the thoughts that surface.
- Read books and articles as a family on some aspect of spirituality and discuss them.
- Take time to practice the family values by working with others in need and discuss the experience.
- Spend time as a family discussing spirituality and how this integrates into daily life.

Children benefit from expanding their perspectives of the world. A child's spirituality will help make sense of the world and all of its good and bad experiences. Children who have no anchor on which to tie their beliefs are often lost and confused when faced with a life-changing experience such as the death of a family member or another family crisis. Parents provide children with this anchor by sharing spiritual beliefs with them and allowing their children to grow in their beliefs.

Children will reach a point where they question the spiritual beliefs taught to them by their parents. They will ultimately incorporate what their parents have taught them with their own experience of the world which will result in ownership of their own beliefs. These children will ultimately build their foundation for adulthood on these newly defined beliefs.

Parents are instilled with the responsibility of sharing a spiritual belief with their children and teaching them values by which to guide their lives. Children need a strong foundation on which to rely as they experience the world around them and discover their purpose, and they need clear values by which to make choices and live their lives. Parents who provide this support for their children will give their children the tools and guidance needed to create successful and happy lives.

25

Remain in Constant Amazement at the Miracle of Your Child

Mark: You want to come over to my house after school? My parents are out of town.

Jack: Where are they?

Mark: In Europe. They'll be gone a couple of weeks.

Jack: Is anyone staying with you?

Mark: Yeah, my nanny. But, she doesn't really care what I do. My parents leave all of the time, and as long as I go to school and stay out of trouble, she leaves me alone.

Jack: Yeah, my parents left once for a couple of weeks and they never came back.

Mark: What do you mean?

Jack: They went to Florida, and they left me with my grandmother. I was supposed to move there with them at the end of the school year, but they never came back to get me.

Mark: Do you ever see them?

Jack: I talk to them every once in a while on the phone, but I don't really care anymore. I'll just live with my grandmother.

Mark: Looks like we got the freedom that most kids dream about! No parents to constantly harass us to behave and tell us to do good in school. We're lucky.

Jack: (sadly) Yeah, we're lucky.

The rules change when a child is born. Parents can no longer think of their needs first; the needs of the child take precedence. This is a choice a parent makes when accepting a child into his or her life. Putting the needs of a child first can be a challenge when one is struggling to make sense of life; find a balance between work and play; or redefine self. Yet these challenges need to be processed within the parameters of the family. Parents cannot leave their children while they "find themselves" or try to recapture their youth. A child who experiences the confusing absence of a parent--whether for a week, months or years--cannot make sense of the parent's need to leave. All the child knows is that the parent is no longer at home when the day ends. The child is left to wonder what he or she could have done differently so the parent would not have left. Even if the parent returns, the trust and safety that existed between the parent and child is damaged, as the child does not know if the time will come again when the parent needs space and decides to leave.

Likewise, parents are not supposed to give back children. Children are not objects that can be returned or thrown away if they no longer fit into the parents' lifestyles. I have many students who do not live with their parents. I can no longer assume that when I contact a child's guardian I will be talking to the parent. When I ask students where their parents are, these are common responses.

- Mom is working out of town. She comes home on the weekends.
- Dad is in prison.
- Mom lives with her boyfriend and his kids.
- I don't know where my dad is. I last saw him when I was six years old.

- My mom left the house on Saturday night, and she never came home.
- My parents are living in Mexico right now.

Parents should be in awe of the miracle of having children, yet children are becoming an inconvenience for many parents. Children are interfering with jobs, relationships, addictions and the freedom to have fun. Many adults neglect their role as a parent when they commit an illegal act and end up in prison; when they work in a job that only allows them to see their children a few hours a week; when they spend time with a hobby that replaces time with their children; when they choose an addiction to drugs or alcohol over being a parent; or when they choose the demands of a new relationship over the demands of being a parent. Children internalize a parent's neglect and begin to believe that it is their own fault. Children, in their young minds, reason that if a parent is not available to them there is something wrong with them as children. These children believe their own behaviors, appearance, personality or actions keep their parents away. Children learn to believe if they were different, their parents would spend more time with them. Children expand this reasoning to believe that if their own parents do not want to be with them, there is something inherently wrong with them and no one will ever want to be with them. This belief taints every relationship that these children will have in the future, and it will plant the seed for abusive relationships, addictions and destructive choices. These children often end up in alternative schools or a detention facility because their hunger for attention causes them to engage in attention-getting destructive behaviors. The parent/child relationship is the most crucial relationship children have because it is the foundation for all future relationships.

A fundamental element of the parent/child relationship is the parent's attitude towards the child. If children are treated as a burden, then children will grow-up believing that they do not have the right to take up space in the world. This destructive belief can lead to depression, addictions and unhealthy choices. When children believe that their parents treasure every day spent with them, then they grow-up believing that they have value and worth. These children will learn to treat themselves with dignity. Children soak up all of the attention, love and care that parents can give them. Children crave knowing that they matter and that their parents cherish them. Children might take parents to their limits with patience, trust and energy, but the love and care parents feel towards their children should always be evident. If a parent is no longer able to see his or her child as a miracle and a gift and the parent is no longer enamored with the child, guidance from a counselor, minister or another professional is recommended. The parent/child relationship is out of balance, and an objective third party will help restore the balance of the relationship. This is essential for the child's healthy development and success.

You are your child's primary support, cheerleader, safety net, and love. Your ability to recognize the miracle of your child—regardless of the daily challenges your child might bring you—will send a message to your child that he or she has the right to be here and accomplish great things. Your child will know that you are grateful for being his or her parent, and thus, your child will have the foundation needed to reach for his or her full potential. Stay in constant amazement at the miracle of your child. Let your child know that he or she is a true gift for you, and you are thankful for the opportunity to be his or her parent.

CONCLUSION

All children can be successful. All children, regardless of the challenges they face with poverty, home instability, learning struggles, outside influences or personal issues have the resources to become a success. The Search Institute in Minneapolis, MN conducts research to determine what children need to achieve success. Their research resulted in the 40 Developmental Assets that define the experiences and characteristics young people need to develop into healthy adults. These assets are external such as having a supportive family and participation in youth programs, and they are internal such as having a sense of purpose and being motivated to achieve. The research conducted by the Search Institute has shown that all children can be successful. All children, despite the challenges encountered in their young lives, have the ability to do well. All children have some positive assets that will help them achieve. A child's economic situations, home life, learning challenges, outside influences, or personal difficulties do not determine his or her potential for success. When a child identifies his or her positive assets and enhances them, success is possible. When adults in the lives of a child—especially parents—focus on developing positive assets in a child, the child can find success. More positive assets lead to more opportunities for success. Essentially, all children have the resources to be successful, but they need adults in their lives to teach them to use the resources to achieve success. Additionally, the involvement of adults, more specifically parents, in a child's life has a profound impact on the child's opportunities for success. More information about the research of the Search Institute and a list of the

40 Developmental Assets can be found on their website www.search-institute.org.

The research of the Search Institute shows that adult involvement in a child's life greatly enhances a child's opportunities for achievement and success. A child who does not have involved adults can still succeed, but it will be a challenge. Most children are not equipped for this challenge. No other adult can have the same level of impact on your child than you do. Involvement in your child's life includes spending time with your child, talking to your child, being involved in your child's school and activities, and staying connected to your child's emotional development.

Be proactive in your child's education and stay connected to your child. Work with your child and the school to ensure that your child will achieve success in school. Parents and schools are partners in the healthy development of children, but you are the fundamental guide in your child's success. The quality of your relationship with your child is the key to keeping your child safe, healthy and successful. Our world is filled with young minds containing the potential to create miracles. Our job as adults is to cultivate and nurture this potential so that children can grow into successful, happy and purposeful members of society. Children need to be prepared to be active and contributing participants in society. Your child has the power to positively transform the world, and your involvement in your child's life will ignite this power. Stay connected and involved with your child as your child grows. The quality of your relationship with your child is the key to his or her success and happiness.

Disclaimer

The information shared by Michelle Farias is for educational purposes, and it is not a substitute for professional counseling or medical advice. This publication is sold with the understanding that the author is not engaged in rendering medical, health or any other type of professional services in the book. The reader of this publication should consult with a mental health or medical professional for concerns related to his or her (or his or her child's) specific situation or condition. The author specifically disclaims all responsibility for any liability, loss, or risk, personal or otherwise, which is incurred as a consequence, directly or indirectly, from the use and application of any contents of this book.

REFERENCES

Centers for Disease Control and Prevention. *Surveillance* Summaries, May 21, 2004. MMWR 2004:53 (No. SS-2).

Department of Health and Human Services (2002). *Child Abuse and Neglect Fatalities: Statistics and Interventions.* Retrieved October 15, 2004, from http://nccanch.acf.hhs.gov

Egley, A. & Major, A. (2004). *Highlights of the 2002 National Youth Gang Survey.* U.S. Department of Justice: Office of Juvenile Justice and Delinquency Prevention.

U.S. Department of Education. (2001). *Students Whose Parents Did Not Go To College* (Office of Educational Research and Improvement), Washington D.C.

U.S. Department of Health and Human Services. *Take Action Against Bullying,* [Brochure]. Available at 1-800-789-2647.

U.S. Department of Health and Human Services. *Tips for Teens,* [Brochure]. Available at 1-800-487-4889.

FREE PARENT CONSULTATION

Michelle Farias offers parents the innovative service of a *Parent Coach*. Ms. Farias provides parents with objective and insightful feedback on the challenging task of raising children in today's society. Ms. Farias works with parents individually through telephone consultations to help guide them through the obstacles and doubts that all parents experience when raising children. This service is for parents of children from infants through young adulthood.

If you are interested in receiving a free introductory 30 minute coaching session with Ms. Farias, email her at information@succeedinschool.com or call 1-800-405-2771 to request more information.

FREE AUDIO CD

Michelle Farias' seminars are available through audio CDs. Timely topics are discussed covering the various issues parents face while raising children in today's society.

If you are interested in receiving a free copy of one of Ms. Farias' CDs, email information@succeedinschool.com or call 1-800-405-2771 to request more information.

FREE PARENT INFORMATION

Michelle Farias wants parents to be able to stay up-to-date on current issues related to children's health and safety. Her monthly parent email alerts discuss the most current topics for today's youth. Email information@succeedinschool.com to request a subscription for these informative parent alerts.

PARENT ON PURPOSE™
SEMINARS

Michelle Farias brings her insightful and entertaining message to parents through her *Parent on Purpose* Seminars. Her most popular seminar

Lunch For Your Kids™

is conducted for corporations during employee lunches. Seminars are also available for organizations. For more information about booking a seminar, contact us at information@succeedinschool.com or call 1-800-405-2771.

Printed in the United States
83663LV00005B/365/A